Professional Ethics and Practice in Organizational Development

Professional Ethics and Practice in Organizational Development

A Systematic Analysis of Issues, Alternatives, and Approaches

Louis P. White
Kevin C. Wooten

PRAEGER

PRAEGER SPECIAL STUDIES • PRAEGER SCIENTIFIC

New York • Philadelphia • Eastbourne, UK
Toronto • Hong Kong • Tokyo • Sydney

Library of Congress Cataloging in Publication Data

White, Louis P.
   Professional ethics and practice in
organizational development.

   Bibliography: p.
   Includes indexes.
   1. Organizational change.   2. Professional
ethics.   3. Organizational change--Moral and
ethical aspects.   I. Wooten, Kevin C.   II. Title.
HD58.8.W48   1985   658.4'06   85-9523
   ISBN 0-03-004222-4 (alk. paper)

Published and Distributed by the
Praeger Publishers Division
(ISBN Prefix 0-275)
of Greenwood Press, Inc.,
Westport, Connecticut

Published in 1986 by Praeger Publishers
CBS Educational and Professional Publishing, a Division of CBS Inc.
521 Fifth Avenue, New York, NY 10175 USA

© 1986 by Praeger Publishers

6789   052   987654321

Printed in the United States of America on acid-free paper

INTERNATIONAL OFFICES

Orders from outside the United States should be sent to the appropriate address listed below. Orders from areas not listed below should be placed through CBS International Publishing, 383 Madison Ave., New York, NY 10175 USA

Australia, New Zealand
Holt Saunders, Pty. Ltd., 9 Waltham St., Artarmon, N.S.W. 2064, Sydney, Australia

Canada
Holt, Rinehart & Winston of Canada, 55 Horner Ave., Toronto, Ontario, Canada M8Z 4X6

Europe, the Middle East, & Africa
Holt Saunders, Ltd., 1 St. Anne's Road, Eastbourne, East Sussex, England BN21 3UN

Japan
Holt Saunders, Ltd., Ichibancho Central Building, 22-1 Ichibancho, 3rd Floor, Chiyodaku, Tokyo, Japan

Hong Kong, Southeast Asia
Holt Saunders Asia, Ltd., 10 Fl, Intercontinental Plaza, 94 Granville Road, Tsim Sha Tsui East, Kowloon, Hong Kong

Manuscript submissions should be sent to the Editorial Director, Praeger Publishers, 521 Fifth Avenue, New York, NY 10175 USA

In memory of
Dorothy Harlow
Mentor and friend

Preface

With the increasing complexity of problems experienced by today's modern organizations, the field of OD is experiencing significant growth. Moreover, OD is rapidly being included as an integral part of organizational goal achievement. Organizations are creating departments to handle this function, as well as increasing their use of external change agents. Many colleges of business and schools of industrial/organizational psychology have developed and currently offer courses in OD. Some institutions now offer degrees in the field.

Along with the increasing importance of OD as a separate discipline, increased attention is being given to the ethical issues in the field of OD, and to professional ethics in general. Accrediting agencies for colleges of business now require that specific attention be given to business ethics as part of nearly all undergraduate and graduate curriculum. Likewise, departments of industrial/organizational psychology are required by the American Psychological Association to deal with ethical considerations as part of degree programs. Each of these areas has chosen to deal with the subject of ethics at a microlevel, that is, on an individual discipline level. This method totally neglects a systematic approach to the study of professional ethics in general and to OD specifically.

A major reason for neglecting the study of ethics is that there are no texts available that deal with professional ethics, nor are there any such texts that deal with the ethics of OD.

For the first time a systematic and analytical approach to professional ethical systems in general, and the ethics of OD specifically is provided. The basic position taken by the writers is that professional ethics can be dealt with from an "action research" perspective. As the detailed table of contents shows, the book deals with the ethics and practice of OD from both a descriptive and prescriptive approach.

The primary target market is schools of business for both graduate and undergraduate training. Psychology departments that offer Industrial Organizational Psychology programs would also be users. Other potential markets include Schools of Public Administration, Human Resource Development, and practicing consultants.

This book provides the necessary models and other techniques to study the question of ethics in a systematic, analytical, and scientific way.

Chapter 1 provides a brief history of the development of the field of OD and its current status, by focusing upon the development of OD as a profession. Chapter 2 deals with the education and training of the practitioner and the influence of values on theory and practice.

Chapter 3 discusses professional ethics by delineating its parameters relative to the philosophical study of ethics. The discussion deals with ethical systems and the stages of their evolution. This approach provides a framework for the assessment of where OD is in its development.

Chapter 4 uses role theory to analyze the OD process. The impact of roles on the change effort is discussed by looking at the individual and mutual roles of the change agent and client system as the OD process proceeds through the various stages. Chapter 5 deals with the client-consultant relationship by looking at factors that influence the change relationship. The idea of change agent/client system maturity is introduced and the consequences of a mature change relationship are assessed.

Chapter 6 deals with ethical dilemmas in the field of OD. An ethical dilemma is defined and ethical dilemmas are categorized. A model for the study of ethical dilemmas is developed as a means of analyzing where and how in the OD process specific dilemmas occur. Chapter 7 assesses a representative sample of existing codes of ethics, relative to their coverage of major ethical dilemma categories. An important point of this chapter is that regardless of the rate of development of existing codes, the occurrence of ethical dilemmas can best be dealt with through a mature change relationship.

Chapter 8 discusses the future of OD. Methods of developing a science of change are discussed and suggestions for developing OD as a profession are offered. A method is proposed to develop an ethical system for the profession that will take into account ethical dilemmas of the present as well as the questions that will confront the profession in the future.

Acknowledgments

The major reason for writing *Professional Ethics and Practice in Organizational Development* was to stimulate discussion about the ways in which the ethics of a profession influence and interact with the practice of that profession. The models presented throughout the book help provide a systematic approach to the exploration of that process. Hopefully, the process of developing a comprehensive code of ethics for the field of OD will be enhanced somewhat.

While the authors are solely responsible for the final product, there are several people who assisted in the project. Kathleen Ensenat Sparks edited and corrected the final copy. The project would not have begun had it not been for our secretary, Kathy Hurkmans. Thanks are due to Dr. Mark Frankel of the IIT Center, Chicago, Illinois, and Dr. Terry Cobb of Virginia Polytechnical Institute and State University for their comments and suggestions; and Dr. James Galtney for being an appropriate role model of a consultant. Many thanks to Tom Burke for years of support and constant encouragement. Thanks also to Dean Rosemary Pledger, School of Professional Studies, for her support throughout the project. Our family members, Chris and Mary Helen Wooten and Matthew White, deserve our gratitude for their patience and understanding. Special recognition is given to Joanne Ferencsik.

Contents

Professional Ethics and Practice in Organizational Development

1

The Past and Present
of Organizational
Development

INTRODUCTION

In the investigation of professional ethics and issues surrounding professional practice in Organizational Development (OD), several preliminary issues must be dealt with. First, what exactly is OD, and what isn't it. Due to OD's rapid evolution and contemporary popularity, can OD be considered a legitimate profession and a science? Specifically, what are the characteristics that have led to its present status? This chapter will attempt a contemporary definition of OD, based on its historical development, both professionally and technologically. This chapter will also attempt to review OD's present status and highlight its current operational difficulties from the perspective of practitioners, consumers, and theorists.

HISTORY AND GROWTH OF OD

OD in General

The rapid growth and development of today's organizations has been accompanied by growth in attending industries and disciplines. An area where growth has burgeoned has been OD. This attendant growth has received primary inputs from the changing environment. The role of change in science, the economy, the legal environment, and individual needs and expectations has placed a high value on the ability of an organization to adapt to these changing conditions. In today's world of multinational corporations, the decline in natural resources, a changing composition in the workforce, political upheaval, and the threat of nuclear war, life for the individual has become an organizational one, however defined. As noted by Huse (1980) "we live in a world of organizations, we are born, educated, live, work, and die in organizations. Each of us is involved in a number of different organizations regardless of what we do, whether at work or play" (p. 17).

The question of balance between individual and organizational needs and goals dominates the very essence of modern existence, present and future. Adaptability of the individual to the organization and the organization's adaptability to the individual are subsequently the mainstays for human survival. The need for both individual and organizational adaptability comes at a time when human systems themselves are in a period of remarkable transition. The growth in knowledge and technology has induced change from an industrial society to a postindustrial one based on information and services. Contemporary observers such as Toffler (1980) and Naisbitt (1982) foresee this postindustrial era as a highly turbulent period, with exponential societal, organizational, and individual transitions occurring.

The relationship between the organization and the individual is ultimately a question of mutual adaptability. Figure 1.1 shows the relationship among these factors. This adaptability is not an inherent feature of organizations. On the contrary, organizations have turned to organizational development experts as a means of acquiring the ability to deal with change. As shown, the human resource enters the organization, an ongoing system. Within this system, the human resource must adapt to the ongoing social process and become part of it. These social and human processes interact with and are part of the organization's structure and technology. The results of this confluence of inputs, processes, and interactions are unique organizational and individual outputs.

The primary objective of OD then is to create an organizational environment where these organizational and individual outputs can be maximized. Indeed, it is a rare organization that innately possesses the capability to maximize these outputs. Normally, organizations focus on maximization of organizational outputs without a full understanding of the roles played by the individual within them. This

FIG. 1.1. The Organization's Internal Environment of Technology

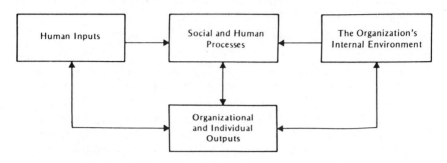

Source: From Beer, M. "The Technology of Organization Development." In M. D. Dunnette (ed.), *Handbook of Industrial and Organizational Psychology.* Chicago: Rand McNally, 1976, p. 958.

traditional approach taken by most organizations requires that OD expand and that advocates guide the development of organizations to a point where mutual adaptability between individual and organizational outputs occur simultaneously.

Assuming that organizational flexibility and the capability of responding to internal and external stimuli to change is not an innate characteristic of traditional organizations, OD is one available alternative. The adaptability and flexibility as a result of OD is a quality that is learned by organizational participants who through the newly acquired phenomenon of change advocacy, are able to meet the challenges of modern organizational environments. The range of values, philosophies, and methods—indeed, the science of OD—has become an ongoing evolutionary process. While there is general consensus as to the purpose, values, and methods involved in OD, its philosophical, technological, and ethical development continue as matters for further study.

Given the context of OD's primary objective, what then is an adequate definition of the concept or term, and what are some of its basic characteristics? The term organizational development when accepted at face value could refer to many different approaches to organizational improvement. However, during the past decade, scholars, practitioners, and consumers of OD have developed a more refined sense of what the field contributes. A major factor that detracts significantly from the specificity of what exactly OD is, comes from the notion that OD is still evolving and developing. Indeed, the parameters of OD are not clear, although some commonality does exist.

Consider the following contemporary definitions:

> Bennis (1963) sees OD as: "A deep concern with applying social science knowledge to create more viable social systems; a commitment to action, as well as to research" (p. 157).
>
> Beckhard (1969) conceptualizes OD as: "An 'effort' (1) planned, (2) organization wide, and (3) managed from the top to, (4) increase effectiveness and health through, (5) planned interventions in the organization's processes, using behavior science knowledge" (p. 9).
>
> French and Bell (1978) define OD as: "A long range effort to improve an organization's problem-solving and renewal processes, particularly through more effective and collaborative management of organization culture—with special emphasis on the culture of formal work teams—with the assistance of a change agent, or catalyst, and the use of the theory and technology of applied behavioral science, including action research" (p. 14).
>
> Huse (1980) defines OD as: "A process by which behavioral science principles and practices are used in an ongoing organization in a planned and systematic way to attain such goals as developing greater competence, bringing about organizational improvement, improvement in the quality of worklife, and improving organizational effectiveness" (p. 3).
>
> Lippitt (1982) sees OD as: "Any planned, organization-wide effort to increase the effectiveness and health of organizations through various intervention in the organizational processes using behavioral and management sciences technologies" (p. 10).

Similarly, there is some commonality in what characteristics shape the field of OD. French and Bell (1973) allude to seven characteristics which differentiate organizational development from more traditional interventions. These seven are: "(1) an emphasis, although not exclusively so, on group and organizational processes in contrast to substantive content; (2) an emphasis on the work team as the key unit for learning more effective modes of organizational behavior; (3) an emphasis on the collaborate management of work team culture; (4) an emphasis on the management of the culture of the total system and to the total system ramifications; (5) the use of the action research model; (6) the use of a behavior scientist change agent, or catalyst; and (7) a view of the changes effort as an ongoing process" (p. 19–20).

Very closely related are the specification of characteristics as developed by Wexley and Yukl (1977). They developed thirteen common characteristics which are reflected in most OD efforts. These are:

"(1) it involves a total organizational system; (2) it views organizations from a systems approach; (3) it is supported by top management; (4) the services of a third party change agent is often used; (5) OD is a planned effort; (6) it is intended to increase organizational competence and health; (7) using behavioral science knowledge; (8) it is a relatively long-term process; (9) it is an ongoing process; (10) it mainly focuses on changing the attitudes, behavior, and performance of organizational groups or teams rather than individuals; (11) it relies primarily on experiential as opposed to didactic learning; (12) it uses an action research intervention model; and (13) it emphasizes the importance of goal setting and planning action" (p. 335–37).

While the perceptions of what OD is may vary slightly, there are apparent threads of commonality. As defined herein, OD is a process that (1) occurs within the organization over a long period of time; and (2) takes place within, among, and around organizational participants and subsystems (human, technological, and structural). *Within* refers to intrapersonal change and growth, *among* refers to an interpersonal component, and *around* refers to a development of the interactional processes that occur between the individual, the workgroup, and the organizational technology and structure. (3) OD is inclusive, in that for an intervention to be effective, all members of the organization must be involved. (4) OD involves an action-research orientation, requiring the application of the scientific method to practical organizational problems with the objective of developing the problem-solving capabilities of organizational participants. (5) OD is aimed at personal, professional, organizational, and societal dignity, growth, competence, and freedom; and (6) it is guided by a change agent, whose major function is to act as a catalyst in this dynamic process.

Historical Perspective and Evolution

The history and evolution of OD is one that relatively little is written about. French and Bell (1972) and Huse (1980) have treated the subject, making note of the major trends and the scholars and practitioners responsible for them. Without question, the early pioneers of the profession have significantly shaped it and influenced its humanistic orientation for years to come. A review of the literature reveals that the history and events leading up to the development of the OD profession have two distinct sources of influence. These two sources are laboratory training and survey feedback.

Laboratory training, or t-groups, began from attempts using unstructured small-group situations allowing participants to learn from their own interactions with others. One of the first attempts at using this form of learning resulted in the establishment of the National Training Laboratories, or NTL, in Bethel, Maine. According to accounts by Bradford (1967), and Marrow (1967), the NTL was a result of efforts to use group study workshops which began in the summer of 1946 at the State Teachers College at New Britain, Connecticut. This program was part of an effort sponsored by the Research Center for Group Dynamics, at that time located at the Massachusetts Institute of Technology. The members of this team included Kurt Lewin, Ronald Lippitt, Leland Bradford, and Kenneth Benne.

With permanent establishment of the NTL, experimentation of t-groups progressed through the late forties. During the 1950s, application of laboratory training spread into organizations. Early practitioners such as McGregor, Shepard, and Blake were among the first to apply laboratory training to ongoing systems. According to French and Bell (1972) and Huse (1980), McGregor, while working with Union Carbide in 1957, was the first to hurdle the problem of transferring the t-group process to industry. At approximately the same time, Shepard began work with ESSO Standard Oil, where he initiated t-group activities at refineries located in Baton Rouge, Bayonne, and Bayway. During this time, Robert Blake joined the effort, and use of laboratory instrumentation was implemented, based on work by Jane Mouton at the University of Texas.

The second major historical impetus for organizational development is that of survey research. Survey research, which is a form of action research, utilizes attitude surveys, and efforts to feedback results to organizational participants. As noted by French and Bell (1973), the history of survey research revolves around the activities of members of the Research Center for Group Dynamics, which moved to the University of Michigan shortly after Kurt Lewin's death in 1947. According to Marrow (1969), several of the key members of this group included Festinger, Lippitt, McGregor, French, Cartwright, and Deutsh. Joining these scholars later were Mann and Likert.

Survey research was legitimately implemented in 1948–50 at the Detroit Edison Company by Floyd Mann. This effort involved feedback of a companywide survey to groups and departments of employees. Because of the success of these "interlocking chains of conferences" as described by Mann, much credence was given to the survey research method. As such, this method, as a form of action research, has significantly influenced the shape and direction of contemporary OD.

Given the two early efforts in OD, that of t-groups and survey research, the evolution of OD as a discipline can be traced. Figure 1.2

FIG. 1.2. Stages of Development of the Organizational Development Science and Profession

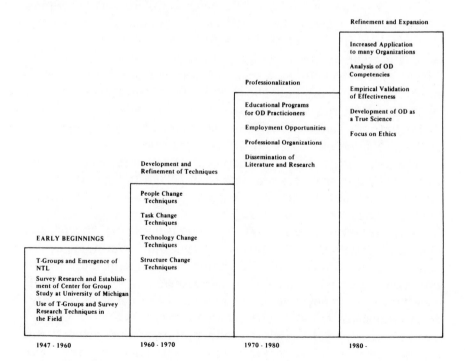

depicts four distinct stages of development of OD as a science and as a profession. These four stages are: (1) early beginnings; (2) development and refinement of techniques; (3) professionalization; and (4) refinement and expansion. Although dates are associated with each stage, the actual beginning and ending of each stage is highly disputable.

The period 1947–60 encompasses the work of the early pioneers. It was marked by the work of Lewin, Lippitt, Bradford, and Benne at the National Training Labs, where the t-group efforts were developed. Additionally, Mann, and later Likert at the University of Michigan, using survey feedback contributed significantly. As well, efforts through the 1960s involving the application of t-groups, survey research, and other similar techniques are included. This early stage then can be described as OD's earliest conceptual development and experimentation in the field.

The second stage of development in OD shown by Figure 1.2, is characterized by the development and refinement of OD technologies. This stage occurred roughly until the 1970s, with many of these efforts still occurring. Here, the development of various techniques progressed and evolved. The emergence of popular OD techniques such as transactional analysis, management by objectives, job enrichment, grid-training, matrix design, sociotechnical systems, etc., were evident. These techniques were developed and refined to assist in inducing needed changes in people, the nature of work, organizational technology, and organizational structure. This stage is typified by efforts to apply various behavioral science techniques to a myriad of organizational problems in a rapidly changing environment.

The third stage in the development of organizational development is shown as professionalization (Fig. 1.2). Although evidence of parts of this stage are noticeable in the 1960s, this stage finally emerged during the 1970s. Like the second stage of development, professionalization in many respects is still occurring. Indeed, the emergence of graduate programs and programs of continuing education aimed specifically at the OD profession are evident. The 1970s witnessed a tremendous growth in employment opportunities for OD practitioners, be they internal or external consultants. Many large organizations created staff OD functions during this time. Concurrently, professional organizations also blossomed during the 1970s, with a tremendous rise in the number of practitioners, and those wishing to become practitioners. Without question, the 1970s witnessed a deluge of literature and research in the form of journal articles and books. This third stage was, and still is, typified by efforts to create an identity for the OD field.

The fourth stage in the development of OD is characterized as refinement and expansion (Fig. 1.2). This stage is shown to include the increased application of OD to many organizations. During this time, all organizations, big or small, prosperous or not, have accessibility to OD services and programs. This period can be shown to involve an increased effort to determine OD competencies for OD practitioners. Specifically, increased efforts at showing bottom-line results and legitimate behavior change can be seen as more scientific approaches to OD are included. Based on the concern for professionalization, an increased focus on professional ethics also can be observed. Thus, the stage of refinement and expansion is typified by attempts to provide effective OD services to all organizations, through effective means, by competent practitioners.

CURRENT STATUS OF OD AND ITS PROBLEMS

Professional and Technological Developments

The last two decades have witnessed tremendous professional and technological developments in the OD discipline. OD's current status has been inextricably shaped by the stages of evolution through which it has progressed. Currently, OD, given its rapid development and current emphasis, is engaged in professionalization efforts through its refinement and expansion activities. The position in which OD finds itself professionally and technologically can be seen as a direct correlate to its rapid development. In their review of the literature, Friedlander and Brown (1974) note that "today OD is emerging as a field of interdisciplinary academic study and as a recognized profession" (p. 314). Friedlander and Brown base their conclusion on the increased number of practitioners in the field, accrediting efforts for practitioners, professional associations, and the number of books and articles published in the field.

Friedlander and Brown's optimism is, however, not totally shared. Alderfer and Berg (1977) note that "whether one observes OD from inside or out, there is ambivalence about whether the field is or should be called a profession. Among themselves practitioners are unsure what they wish to take with respect to educational requirements, ethical standards, and the discipline of members" (p. 90). Thus, one can certainly conclude that OD is in a state of change. Recently Kegan (1983) reflected that

> To continue the professionalization of organization development (OD) practice, OD needs both greater differentiation and greater integration. OD needs cross-fertilization with traditional organizational functions. . . . The OD community needs to continue developing its knowledge of itself, collaboration among OD associations, and academic practitioner coordination. OD needs to extend both its inclusiveness and its power. (p. 19)

Although there is considerable debate as to OD's exact status, Friedlander and Brown's (1974) thesis can certainly be supported in terms of numbers alone. Huse (1980) notes the growth in the OD network, a professional association, from 200 members in 1970 to 1300 members in 1979. Kegan (1982) in a survey of OD practitioners reported that over half of the OD Network members have joined within three years. Similiar increases are as well noted by the OD Division of the Academy of Management, and the Division of Industrial and Organizational Psychology of the American Psychological Association.

What then has caused this tremendous growth in the OD profession? Beckhard (1969) sees this growth directly related to significant changes in various environments, new knowledge, and new managerial strategies that are required. Environmental changes noted by Beckhard (1969), Bennis (1969), Huse (1980), as well as Lippitt (1982) include such factors as the effects from the knowledge and technological explosion, economic uncertainty, instantaneous communications, multinational organizations, shortened product life cycles, built in obsolescence, changing composition of the work force, and concern for social and cultural issues.

In addition to changing environmental conditions, four other significant changes have provided the necessary impetus for the professional development of the OD field. These changes include a change in values, the change in the nature of work, outdated organizational structures, and mismanagement. Contemporary efforts emphasizing individualism/autonomy, knowledge versus authority-based management, and the right to grow and develop have caused a tremendous shift in ideologies (Martin and Lodge, 1975). The nature of work too has been transformed in the last two decades from a production based economy to a service based economy, with an information based economy now developing. In today's workworld, with the advent of the home computer, there is concern for not only "how" work is done but "where" it is done.

The highly structured bureaucratic organizations have not been able to respond quickly and adequately enough to both individual members, and to the general population, thereby creating a tremendous need for OD services. Authors such as Argyris (1957) and Bennis (1966) have long argued that mature individuals and a complex society could not be best served by the bureaucratic tradition, although many of our most critical institutions have remained bureaucratic in nature and form. All of the previously mentioned changes culminate in the problem of mismanagement. According to Hirschowtiz (1974), mismanagement has been caused by such factors or managerial failures to appreciate complexity, failures to make investments in human assets, and using out-dated theories of motivation, to name a few.

How then has OD responded professionally to changes in the environment, values, the nature of work, bureaucratic structure, and mismanagement? Statistics about professional organizations, employment opportunities, educational programs, and abundance of the literature tell only part of the story. The other part of the story is the tremendous proliferation of OD technologies. Naisbitt (1982) has noted that there are three stages in technological innovation. He states "First, the new technology on invention will follow the line of least resistance, second, the technology is used to improve previous technology, and third, new directions or uses are discovered that grow out of the technology itself" (p. 27). OD has progressed from the first stage and is now in the second stage. In its first stage, OD was based in learning institutes such as NTL, which people attended for personal gain (in the line of least resistance). Later, OD has now been applied to the management of organizations, thereby hopefully improving the way we have done things in the past.

From the technological growth, numbers of OD programs are now available to address human, structural, technological, and task related variables. Beer (1976) states that

> the field of organizational development has spawned a wide variety of techniques for dealing with organizations as total systems. These tech-

niques, while sometimes hard on previous research and theory, are often the result of creative practitioners responding to a variety of organizational problems and such. They now constitute a growing social technology for intervening in, changing, and developing organization. (p. 939)

As shown in Table 1.1, an overview of change approaches and the effects upon various change variables can now be illustrated (Hellriegel and Slocum, 1979). Thus, organizational interventions today have a tremendous arsenal of technologies to apply to organizations and their systems variables. People-change techniques have been developed such as survey feedback (Taylor and Bowers, 1972; Nadler, 1977), grid development (Blake and Mouton, 1964), transactional analysis (Benne, 1959; Jongeward, 1973), and sensitivity training (Schien and Bennis, 1965; Rogers, 1970). Programs have also been developed that attempt changes in the task, such as behavior modification (Luthans and Kreitner, 1975), autonomous groups (Cummings and Molloy, 1977; Walton, 1977), job enrichment (Herlzberg, 1968; Hackman and Oldham, 1982), and management by objectives (Odiorne, 1965; Carroll and Tosi, 1973). Programs designed to change technological variables have included attempts at changing the type of technology used (Jaffe and Fromken, 1968; Whisler, 1977). Also, the change in organizational structure as an OD technique (Davis and Lawrence, 1977) has been popular.

A critical review of the previously mentioned intervention technology (Beer, 1976; Friedlander and Brown, 1974; Alderfer, 1972; Porras and Berg, 1978; Bowers, 1973) yields considerable debate as to that technology's effectiveness, but it is clear that OD has technologically developed to the point where choices among means are now available. In fact, most interventions are not pure in the sense that they use only one method; rather, they are hybrid in nature. Further, OD has now developed technologically to the point where the units of analysis and the levels of abstraction are becoming increasingly clear.

As shown in Figure 1.3, OD's technology can be depicted in terms of problems to diagnose, the focus of attention and the mode of intervention. As noted by Schmuck and Miles (1976), these intervention modes flow into each other and are not mutually exclusive. They range from soft (person-change) to hard (task oriented or structure changing) in emphasis. A strong OD program will typically

TABLE 1.1. The Impact of Various Change Approaches Upon Major System Variables

Change approaches	Relative direct impact on major system variables			
	People	*Task*	*Technology*	*Structure*
People focus				
Survey feedback	High	Low to moderate	Low	Low to moderate
Grid organization development	High	Low to high	Low	Low to high
Transactional analysis	High	Low	Low	Low
Sensitivity training	High	Low	Low	Low
Task focus				
Behavior modification	Moderate to high	High	Low	Low to moderate
Autonomous groups	Moderate to high	Very high	Low to moderate	Moderate to high
Job enrichment	Moderate to high	Very high	Low to moderate	Low to moderate
Management by objectives	Moderate to high	High	Low	Low
Technology focus				
Mass Production	Low	Moderate to high	Very high	Low to high
Automation	Low	Moderate to high	Very high	Low to high
Structure Focus				
Bureaucracy	Low	Moderate to high	Low	Very high
Matrix	Low to moderate	High	Low	Very high

Source: From Hellriegel, D. and Slocum, J. W. Jr. *Organizational Behavior*, 2d ed. St. Paul: West, 1979, p. 588.

FIG. 1.3. A Scheme for Classifying OD Interventions

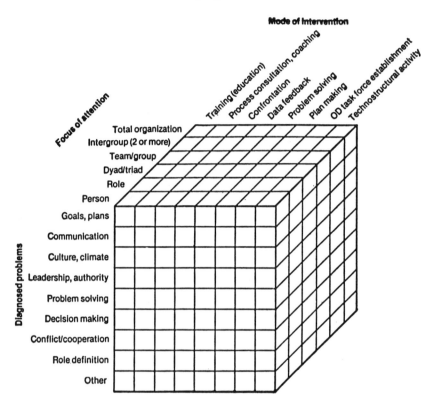

Source: From Schmuck, R. A. and Miles, M. B. (eds.), *Organization Development in Schools*. La Jolla, Cal.: University Associates, 1976, p. 7.

involve all eight components at one time or another. Similar typological models of OD interventions have been developed by Bowers, Franklin, and Pecorella (1975), White and Mitchell (1976), Lippitt and Lippitt (1978), and French and Bell (1978).

The areas where OD has developed technologically, but at a slower rate, are the areas of diagnosis and research/evaluation. A literature review indicates that there are numerous diagnostic methods to be used in OD. Surveys, interviews, observation, secondary data/unobtrusive means have been widely used for more than two decades in OD efforts. As noted by Weisbord (1967) "all four methods of data collection can be used to isolate the two major kinds of discrepancies—between what people say (formal) and what people do (internal), and between what is (organization as it exists) and what ought to be (appropriate environment fit)" (p. 435). Today, interventionists have commercial diagnostic and evaluative instruments such as the Survey of Organizations (Bowers, 1973) as well as methodologies that are experimental in nature to measure their efforts (Campbell and Stanley, 1966). Lippitt (1982) and Stone (1978) have also documented the advantages and disadvantages of these methodologies in applied settings.

There are, however, difficulties with the methodologies for diagnosis as well as evaluation, especially given their use in ever-changing organizations where true effect is difficult to measure. As noted by French, Bell, and Zawacki (1983):

> competent research on the effectiveness of OD is hard to do. . . . It is complicated by a number of characteristics such as the fact that the action program takes place in a real-life, complex social situation, the fact that the goals, interventions, and measurements may change over time. The fact that evaluators may also be program sponsors or advocates; the fact that the program may extend over a long period of time, having ups and downs during that time; and the likelihood that events occurring simultaneously with treatment, the OD program, may also be having profound effects on the outcomes being measured. (p. 20)

Taking professional and technological developments together, OD, like other professions and industries can be analyzed with respect to its life cycle. Utilizing a marketing concept on the developments of the OD profession and its products, Krell (1981) has hypothesized about OD's product life cycle. As shown in Figure 1.4, the OD industry as a whole, mainline OD (comprised of existing techniques such as grid development, MBO, etc.), and traditional OD (t-groups, and action research) can be depicted at five different market stages. These five stages are introduction, growth, maturity, saturation, and decline.

As shown, traditional OD is in the decline stage, whereas mainline OD and OD in general are presently in the saturation stage. Krell argues that the OD industry is moving from the maturity to the saturation stage, and that the packaging of OD will flourish to the point where it will become more easily adopted and copied. He notes that, "in very short order the companies will be unable to distinguish

FIG. 1.4. The Product Life Cycle of OD

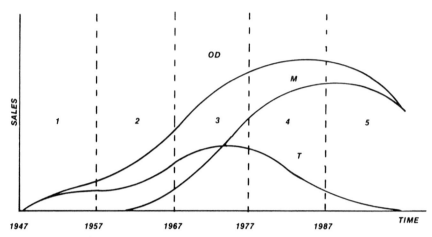

OD The Organization Development Industry as a Whole; M Mainline OD; T Traditional Organization Development

1. Introduction Stage; 2. Growth Stage; 3. Maturity Stage; 4. Saturation Stage; 5. Decline Stage

Source: From Krell, T. C. "The Marketing of Organization Development: Past, Present, and Future." *Journal of Applied Behavioral Science* 17, no. 3, 1981, p. 320.

among the products offered and will accept less individual competence to get technological competence at a good price" (p. 322). Krell makes the point, however, that the saturation period typically occurs over a very long time. Whether or not one agrees with Krell's thesis, the growth in the profession and the seed for its services yields considerable support for his notion concerning the OD industry as a whole.

Critique of the Field

A review of the literature indicates that at present, four major areas in the OD field require attention. These four areas are problems which are recognized stumbling blocks by practitioners, theorists, and consumers alike. The four areas are: (1) the lack of a universal code of ethics and methods for dealing with ethical issues; (2) the lack of generally accepted educational criteria and curriculum; (3) the lack of a unified theory of change; and (4) the lack of longitudinal and evaluation research. Each of these areas, unless dealt with appropriately, will impede OD's continued growth and will threaten its professional and scientific status over the next several decades. At present, due to these difficulties, there is debate as to whether OD is a religious movement (Harvey, 1974), or a new social technology (Havelock, 1972).

The issue of professional ethics has been growing in concern. Contemporary books (Lippitt and Lippitt, 1978; French and Bell, 1978; Huse, 1980; Lippitt, 1982) are now addressing the problem. Recent articles and manuscripts (Walton and Warwick, 1973; Warwick and Kelman, 1973; Pfeiffer and Jones, 1977; Wooten and White, 1983; White and Wooten, 1983) argue that unless the issue of professional ethics is adequately dealt with, the recognition of OD as a profession is in great jeopardy.

A variety of OD theorists and scholars have expressed deep concern over value and ethical problems plaguing the OD field. Walton and Warwick (1973) state the following:

> The rapid expansion of both practice and practitioners in an enchanted field raises numerous ethical questions. Who are its clients and what are its power implications? What measures of professional responsibility should govern the world of the OD practitioner? What are the rights of OD participants, particularly when their power position is weak, vis-à-vis these initiations of change? Is OD a morally neutral tool applicable to any organizational setting, or are these initiations in which its use is ethically questionable? (p. 681)

Pfeiffer and Jones (1977) note the following:

> As the field of human relations training grows and the number of human relations consultants and group facilitation increases, it becomes more important than ever to face the question of ethical behavior. It is necessary to consider with care what is ethical, what is not ethical, and what may be ethical but impossible, imprudent, unprofessional, or incomplete. (p. 217)

Lippitt (1982) reflects that

> Planned change does have ethical implications that should be thoroughly considered by the whole body of practitioners. The moral and ethical

standards that have become involved in this problem of individual and social responsibility should be key to the future advancement in both the private and public sectors of our society. The responsibility for establishing and maintaining high ethical standards rest heavily upon managers and consultants in all kinds of systems. (p. 377)

The problem of ethics in OD is twofold. First, there is the problem of no universal system of ethics to which all practitioners adhere. The growth in the number of practitioners, and the number of professional organizations has yielded considerable heterogeneity of practice and practitioners. (Benne, 1959; Huse, 1980; Lippitt and Lippitt, 1978; Wooten and White, 1983). Although many professional organizations such as the American Psychological Association and the American Society for Training and Development, do have codes of ethics, no one specific association governs the profession and the behavior of all practitioners. This problem is compounded by the fact that anyone, irrespective of education or experience, can enter the field and in many respects consider themselves an OD professional. Consequently, the profession and consumers alike are harmed by those who consciously or unconsciously act less than professionally.

The second concern in the problem of professional ethics involves how practicing consultants and consumers alike resolve the value and ethical dilemmas inherent in complex social and organizational change. The range of issues to be dealt with includes such areas as power, the conflict between values, who is the client, and the target, technical issues such as the appropriateness of the means and methods, confidentiality, manipulation and coercion, cooperation of parties, termination of service, dependency, role contamination, etc. Presently, clients and consumers are left to their own devices when these values and ethical problems arise. As a result much of the impact of an OD intervention is minimized when issues of this nature occur. Chapters 3, 6, and 7 of this book explore these issues fully.

The second major problem in the OD field is the lack of a generally accepted educational criteria and curriculum. Most investigations have discussed the types of competencies required of OD consultants (Warwick and Donoven, 1979; Lippitt and Lippitt, 1978; Menzel, 1975). Books and OD texts such as those by Havelock (1973), Huse (1980), Lippitt (1982), and Albrecht (1982), have as well raised the issue of OD competencies and methods of education and development around them.

Commenting upon the development and training for OD professionals, Alderfer and Berg (1977) note that

> Currently the education and training of OD practitioners is divided between the universities and a variety of ad-hoc temporary systems. The respective strengths and weaknesses of these two types of programs follow closely what one might expect. Outside the University, people are more likely to be exposed to the latest innovations in practice. Inside the University programs are likely to have finer and/or more systematic intellectual bases. Outside programs are more likely to suffer from inadequate or nonexistent intellectual substance. Inside programs are less likely to be current with the latest practical innovations and to provide students with the opportunity to learn from supervised practice of their skills. (p. 93)

Similarly, Lippitt (1982) based on his previous work, notes that

> Unfortunately, the professional development of human system renewal specialists has been a haphazard process. Only recently have workshops, experiences, and courses for developing such skills begun to emerge on a regular basis. (p. 379)

The problem of OD competencies and professional education rest upon two important issues. First is the issue of what exactly is needed in an OD consultant and what are the specific competencies truly required, the mode of acquisition notwithstanding. There is, at present, debate among theorists, educators, practitioners, and consumers as well, as to the specific abilities, skills, knowledge, and behavioral qualities that should be possessed by a competent OD professional. The lack of specificity with regard to competencies and criteria by educators and client systems perpetuates the heterogeneity and divergence of OD consultants' backgrounds. However, until OD is a totally integrated field, such controversy is predictable.

The second issue concerning the competencies and educational criteria problem is the debate concerning the extent to which classroom education versus practical experience produces the best change agent. Almost all critics and experts agree that a broad-based interdisciplinary background is essential. However, the method of learning the application of this knowledge remains unresolved. Lippitt (1982), noting this problem, states that OD practitioners "should be specialists of broad comprehension and ability, rather than merely book-bound manipulation of methods" (p. 361). The problem of change-agent skill, competencies, and development will be specifically addressed in Chapters 2 and 8.

Perhaps the most frequently mentioned problem presently facing the OD field is the lack of a systematic theory of change. Reviews of the literature by Friedlander and Brown (1974), and Alderfer (1976 and 1977) have discussed the absence of an OD theory base. Likewise, contemporary theorists such as Bennis (1969), Burke (1976), and Alderfer (1973) have made note of the problem. Critics such as Strauss (1973), and Levinson (1972) have gone so far as to label OD anti-intellectual and antitheoretical.

Elaborating on the status of OD's lack of a theory base, Friedlander and Brown (1974) state:

> We have generally failed to produce a theory of change which emerges from the change process itself. We need a way of enriching our action synergistically rather that at one or the other experience—to become a science, in which knowledge-getting and knowledge-giving are an integrated process and one that is valuable to all parties involved. We believe that a theory of change must be a theory of practice, which emerges from practice data and is of practice situation, not merely about it. (p. 366)

Further, Burke (1978), noting the need for unity, states the following:

> Even though there is need for a unifying theory, none yet exists. There are a number of theories on which OD is based, but no single theory provides coherence. OD remains a convenient label. We have not progressed beyond Lewin's theoretical steps of unfreezing, changing, and refreezing. (p. 4)

Beer (1976) has also expressed concern toward OD's present state of change theory. He states:

> The field of organizational development tends to be dominated by change efforts which use one technology or one approach to organization change. It still has no established theory for changing organizations or total systems. (p. 984)

At the heart of the controversy concerning a guiding theory of change and a theoretical base is the fact that most of the existing models of the change process do not include all of the participants in the change process, nor all of the stages of change in contemporary efforts. Therefore, most existing theories of change do not visualize both the change agent and the client system as part of a mutual learning process which is organized in steps or stages of transactions and learning. Further, none totally encompasses both total systems and subsystem considerations. The net effect too often therefore is a microtheory of macrochange activity.

Contributing greatly to the problem of a unified change theory is the fact that most investigations have been guided by the particular technology used by the change agent. Most organizational interventions rely heavily upon the techniques used, rather than a theory to guide the actions of the intervention itself. Whether one uses grid development, survey feedback, or management by objectives, the stages of change are determined by the technology surrounding the techniques used, not around a theory of organizational change. This difficulty is treated fully in Chapter 4.

The fourth major problem presently plaguing the OD field is the lack of longitudinal and evaluation research. Similar to the three previous problems discussed, this problem is well documented by contemporary text (French and Bell, 1978; Huse, 1980; Lippitt, 1982), general OD reviews (Alderfer, 1976, 1977; Friedlander and Brown, 1974), and recent reviews of OD research literature (White and Mitchell, 1976; and Porras and Berg, 1978). All of these efforts illustrate what many consider to be the single greatest threat to the OD field for years to come.

From their review of the OD research literature, White and Mitchell (1976) state that

Most OD research uses poor research designs. The measures are subject to halo error and poor reliability. The designs are frequently inadequate for making causal inference. Statistical comparisons are weak and infrequently used. Finally, Hawthorne and experimenter biases effects provide highly plausible alternative hypothesis. (p. 70)

Alderfer (1976), in his review of OD theory and practice states that

The methods of social science are only gradually being adopted for work in more turbulent settings. Systems which defy understanding by practitioners for pragmatic ends tend to be no more accessible to social scientists using rigorous method for scientific ends. Thus, if one may think of OD as having a stable core, where practice has been underway for the longest period of time and a dynamic perimeter whose new developments are taking place, systematic research is more likely in the former than in the latter settings. Accordingly research will tend to lag behind practice in OD as long as the system is organized as it is currently. (p. 220)

Porras and Berg (1978) in their review of the OD research reinforce notions held by White and Mitchell (1976), and Alderfer (1976). They state:

Although a few studies investigating the effects of OD are currently available, little systematic knowledge exists about this body of literature—its size, quality, or generalized findings. Many believe that virtually no research exists and that whatever does exist is not of sufficiently high quality to deserve the title scientific. (p. 249)

There are two overriding reasons for the lack of evaluation research and longitudinal research in OD. The first is that method and tools to conduct longitudinal and evaluation research have only recently been available. Until the last several years, most research designs were applicable only to a stable and controllable environment, or opposed for an everchanging, dynamic, and unpredictable organization. Thus, the research designs and statistical tests used, while although scientifically vigorous, has not been fully applicable to a real-life field context. Much research difficulty concerning the effects of an intervention has been due to faulty design, sources of error, and experimenter biases. Only within the last decade have diagnostic tools been truly scientific, have experimental designs considered the demand characteristics of the organization, and have statistical tests been used to control the effects of moderator variables.

The second reason why evaluation and longitudinal research have caused much concern is the inherent dilemma faced by the interventionist. Change agents are expected to simultaneously engage in two roles, that of practitioner and that of scientist. Unless adequately trained and heavily experienced, practitioners will tend to adopt one of these roles to the exclusion of the other. All too frequently, change agents adopt the role of practitioner to the total exclusion of a research orientation. As a result, many change agents perpetuate the myth that OD is an art rather than a science. Chapters 3 and 8 deal with the issue of OD research in greater depth.

SUMMARY

The field of organizational development can be seen as a relatively new profession, currently in a dynamic state. This chapter has pointed to the need for OD services, illustrating the need for adaptability and flexibility in our contemporary human systems. A definition of OD can now be offered, based on threads of commonality. Such a definition includes the notion that OD involves many organizational subsystems, inclusive of all members, utilizing the scientific approach, emphasizing personal, professional, and organizational growth, competence, and freedom, and is brought about by a highly skilled change agent.

The history and evolution of OD has evolved from two sources, laboratory training and survey feedback. Based on the early work of pioneers such as Lippitt, Lewin, Bennis, Bradford, Shepard, Blake, McGregor, Festinger, French, Cartwright, Deutsh, and Likert, OD's philosophical and methodological approaches were given birth. As a science and a profession, OD can be seen to have progressed through four overlapping stages of development. These four are early beginnings, development and development of techniques, professionalization, and refinement and expansion. Currently, OD is in both of the later two stages.

The professional and technological developments of OD have also been documented, illustrating the marked increase in professional organizations. The changes in the external environment, values, the nature of work itself, and mismanagement can be seen as the impetus for growth. The proliferation of OD techniques, via its technologies, have also been noted. Intervention technologies have been illustrated, which are capable of affecting changes in people, task, organizational structure, and technology. Further, the life cycle of OD's products and services has been illustrated, with its present and future market position in question.

A critique of the OD literature indicates that there are four major concerns in the OD field which, if left unresolved, will deter its continued growth and development. The lack of a universal code of ethics and method for resolving ethical issues, the lack of a unified theory of change, and the lack of longitudinal and evaluative research were discussed. These four problems can be seen as having been caused by such factors as heterogeneity of change agents' background, complexity of issues facing change agents and client systems, confusion over specific change-agent competencies and educational methods, overreliance on techniques rather than theories, narrowly defined change theories, and difficulties in conducting field research.

NOTES

Albrecht, K. *Organization Development: A Total Systems Approach To Positive Change In Any Business Organization.* Englewood Cliffs, N.J.: Prentice-Hall, 1982.

Alderfer, C. P. "Change Processes in Organizations." In M. D. Dunnette (ed.), *Handbook of Industrial and Organizational Psychology.* Chicago: Rand McNally, 1972, 1591-1638.

Alderfer, C. P. "Organizational Development." *Annual Review of Psychology* 25, 1977, 197-233.

Alderfer, C. P. and Berg, D. N. "Organization Development. The Profession and the Practitioner." In P. H. Mirvis and D. N. Berg (eds.), *Failures in Organizational Development and Change.* New York: Wiley Interscience, 1977, 89-104.

Argyris, C. *Personality and Organization.* New York: Harper and Row, 1957.

Beckhard, R. *Organization Development: Strategies and Models.* Reading, Mass.: Addison-Wesley, 1969.

Beer, M. "The Technology of Organizational Development," in M. D. Dunnette (ed.), *Handbook of Industrial and Organizational Psychology.* Chicago: Rand McNally, 1976, 937-94.

Benne, K. D. "Some Ethical Problems in Group and Organizational Consultation." *Journal of Social Issues* 15, 1959, 60-67.

Bennis, W. *Changing Organizations.* New York: McGraw-Hill, 1966.

Bennis, W. *Organization Development: Its Nature, Origin, and Prospects.* Reading, Mass.: Addison-Wesley, 1969.

Bennis, W. G. "A New Role for the Behavioral Sciences: Effecting Organizational Change." *Administrative Science Quarterly*, September, 1965, 124–38.

Berne, E. *Transactional Analysis in Psychotherapy.* New York: Grove Press, 1961.

Blake, R. R. and Mouton, Jane S. *The Managerial Grid.* Houston, Tex.: Gulf Publishing Company, 1964.

Bowers, D. G. "Organizational Development: Promises, Performance, Possibilities." *Organizational Dynamics* 12, 1973, 22–43.

Bowers, D. G., Franklin, J. L. and Pecorella, P. A. "Matching Problems, Precursors, and Interventions in OD: A Systematic Approach." *Journal of Applied Behavioral Science* 11, 1975, 391–409.

Bradford, L. P. "Biography of an Institution." *Journal of Applied Behavioral Science* 3, no. 2, 1967, 145-150.

Burke, W. W. "Organizational Development in Transition." *Journal of Applied Behavioral Science* 12, 1976, 22–43.

Burke, W. W. (ed.) "The Cutting Edge: Current Theory and Practice in Organization Development." La Jolla, Cal.: University Associates, 1978.

Campbell, D. T. and Stanely, J. C. *Experimental and Quasi-Experimental Designs for Research.* Chicago: Rand McNally, 1966.

Carroll, S. and Tosi, H. *Management By Objectives: Applications and Research.* New York: Macmillan, 1973.

Cummings, T. and Molloy, E. *Improving Productivity and the Quality of Life.* New York: Praeger, 1977.

Davis, S. and Lawrence, P. *Matrix.* Reading, Mass.: Addison-Wesley, 1977.

French, W. L. and Bell, C. H. Jr. *Journal of Contemporary Business*, Summer, 1972, 1-8.

French, W. L. and Bell, C. H. Jr. *Organizational Development: Behavioral Science Interventions for Organization Improvement.* Englewood Cliffs, N.J.: Prentice Hall, 1973.

French, W. L. and Bell, C. H. Jr. *Organizational Development: Behavioral Science Interventions for Organization Improvement*, 2d ed., Englewood Cliffs, N.J.: Prentice Hall, 1978.

French, W. L., Bell, C. H. Jr. and Zawacki, R. A. (eds.) *Organizational Development: Theory, Practice, and Research*, rev. ed. Plano, Tex.: Business Publications, 1983.

Friedlander, F. and Brown, L. D. "Organizational Development." *Annual Review of Psychology* 25, 1974, 313-41.

Hackman, J. R. and Oldham, G. R. *Word Redesign.* Reading, Mass.: Addison-Wesley, 1980.

Harvey, J. B. "Organizational Development as a Religious Movement." *Training and Development Journal* 28, no. 3, 1974, 24-27.

Havelock, R. G. *The Change Agent's Guide To Innovation in Education.* Englewood Cliffs, N.J.: Educational Technology Publications, 1973.

Havelock, R. G. "A Critique: Has OD Become A Social Technology?" *Educational Technology* 10, no. 2, 1972, 61-62.

Hellriegel, D. and Slocum, J. W. Jr. *Organizational Behavior*, 2d ed. St. Paul: West, 1979.

Herzberg, F. "One More Time: How Do You Motivate Employees?" *Harvard Business Review* 46, no. 1, 1968, 53-62.

Hirshowitz, R. G. "The Human Aspects of Managing Transition." *Organizational Dynamics* 5, no. 1, 1974, 43-56.

Huse, Edgar F. *Organization Development and Change.* St. Paul: West, 1980.

Jaffe, A. and Fromkin, J. *Technology and Jobs: Automation in Perspective.* New York: Praeger, 1968.

Jones, J. E. and Pfeiffer, J. W. "On the Obsolescence of the Term Organizational Development." *Group and Organization Studies* 2, 1977, 263-64.

Jongeward, D. *Everybody Wins: Transactional Analysis Applied to Organizations.* Reading, Mass.: Addison-Wesley, 1973.

Kegan, D. L. "A Profile of the OD Practitioner." *Group and Organizational Studies* 7, no. 1, 1982, 5-11.

Kegan, D. L. Inclusive Clout: OD's Professional Task. *Organizational Development Journal* 1, no. 1, 1983, 19-22.

Krell, T. C. "The Marketing of Organizational Development: Past, Present, and Future." *Journal of Applied Behavioral Science* 17, no. 3, 1981, 309-323.

Levinson, H. "The Clinical Psychologist as Organizational Diagnostician." *Professional Psychologist* 3, 1972, 34-40.

Lippitt, G. L. and Lippitt, R. *The Consultant Process In Action.* La Jolla, Cal.: University Associates, 1978.

Lippitt, G. L. *Organizational Renewal: A Holistic Approach to Organizational Development*, 2d ed. Englewood Cliffs, N.J.: Prentice-Hall, 1982.

Luthans, F. and Kreitner, R. *Organizational Behavior Modification.* Glenview, Ill.: Scott, Foresman & Co., 1975.

Marrow, A. "Events Leading to the Establishment of the National Training Laboratories." *Journal of Applied Behavioral Science* 3, no. 2, 1967, 145-50.

Martin, W. F. and Lodge, G. C. "Our Society in 1985—Business May Not Like It." *Harvard Business Review*, November-December, 1975, 143-50.

Menzel, R. K. "A Taxonomy of Change Agent Skills." *The Journal of European Training* 4, no. 5, 1975, 289-91.

Nadler, D. *Feedback and Organization Development: Using Data Based Methods.* Reading, Mass.: Addison-Wesley, 1977.

Naisbitt, J. *Megatrends: Ten New Directions Changing Our Lives.* New York: Warner Communications, 1982.

Odiorne, G. S. *Management by Objectives.* New York: Pitman, 1965.

Pfeiffer, J. W. and Jones, J. E. "Ethical Consideration in Consulting." In J. E. Jones and J. W. Pfeiffer (eds.), *The 1977 Annual Handbook for Group Facilitators.* La Jolla, Cal.: University Associates, 1971, 217-25.

Porras, J. I. and Berg, P. L. "Evaluation Methodology in Organizational Development." *Journal of Applied Behavioral Science* 14, no. 2, 1978, 151-73.

Rogers, C. R. *Carl Rogers on Encounter Groups.* New York: Harrow Books, 1970.

Schein, E. and Bennis W. (eds.) *Personal and Organizational Change Through Group Methods: The Laboratory Approach.* New York: John Wiley, 1965.

Schmuck, R. A. and Miles, M. B. (eds.) *Organization Development in Schools.* La Jolla, Cal.: University Associates, 1976.

Stone, E. *Research Methods in Organizational Behavior.* Santa Monica, Cal.: Goodyear Publishing Co., 1978.

Strauss, G. "Organizational Development: Credits and Debits." *Organizational Dynamics* 1, no. 3, 1973, 2-19.

Taylor, J. and Bowers, D. *Survey of Organizations: A Machine Scored Standardized Questionnaire Instrument.* Ann Arbor: University of Michigan Press, 1972.

Toffler, A. *Future Shock.* New York: Random House, 1980.

Walton, R. "Work Innovations at Topeka: After Six Years." *The Journal of Applied Behavioral Science* 13, 1977, 422-33.

Walton, R. E. and Warwick, D. P. "The Ethics of Organizational Development." *Journal of Applied Behavioral Science*, 9, no. 6, 1973, 681-99.

Warwick, D. P. and Donovan, T. "Surveying OD Skills." *Training and Development Journal* 33, no. 9, 1979, 22-25.

Warwick, D. P. and Kelman, H. C. "Ethics in Social Intervention." In G. Zaltman (ed.), *Processes and Phenomena of Social Change.* New York: Wiley Interscience, 1973, 377-449.

Weisbord, M. "Organizational Diagnosis: Six Places to Look for Trouble with or without a Theory." *Group and Organizational Studies*, 1967, December, 430-47.

Wexley, K. N. and Yukl, G. A. *Organizational Behavior and Personal Psychology.* Homewood, Ill.: Richard D. Irwin, 1977.

Whisler, T. "Technology and Organizational Change," in C. Myers, (ed.), *The Impact of Computers on Management.* Cambridge, Mass.: MIT Press, 1967.

White, S. E. and Mitchell, T. F. "Organizational Development: A Review of Research Content and Research Design." *Academy of Management Review* 1, no. 2, 1976, 57-77.

White, L. P. and Wooten, K. C. "Ethical Dilemmas in Various Stages of Organizational Development." *Academy of Management Review*, 8, no. 4, 1983, 690-97.

Wooten, K. C. and White, L. P. "Ethical Problems in the Practice of Organizational Development." *Training and Development Journal* 37, no. 4, 1983, 16-25.

2

The Organizational
Development Profession

INTRODUCTION

Given OD's present status and its current problems, examination of the professionals who compose the field is required to fully understand its nature and context. Each of the four major problems developed in Chapter 1 is at least in part directly related to how OD professionals develop and how they translate their values into thought and action. Although OD is a relatively new profession, the present chapter will investigate the nature of courses in OD, the specific skills and competencies required of a successful practitioner, as well as methods to approach professional development. This chapter will also explore the core values of change agents and of the OD profession, and the ways these values influence the theory and practice of OD.

HOW OD PROFESSIONALS DEVELOP

The OD Career

Reference has been made to various authors (Alderfer and Berg, 1977; and Kegan, 1982) who dispute whether OD is a legitimate profession, and to those who dispute whether OD is a legitimate science (Strauss, 1973; and Levinson, 1972). Irrespective of the position held, the field of OD has grown and will continue to grow over the next several decades. The question of real merit is how will it grow? That is, how will the profession shape itself with respect to professional education and career tracks for practitioners and academicians in a meaningful way? To answer this question, examination of who OD professionals are, and the nature of an OD career is required.

Who are OD professionals? Reference has been to the number of professionals in a variety of OD related groups such as the American Society of Training and Development, the American Psychological Association, the OD Network, etc. The precise determination of the number of actual practitioners belonging to one or more of these associations is difficult to determine. Kegan (1982) investigated the OD Network by analyzing demographic characteristics, internal vs. external affiliation, time usage, job satisfaction and stress, training and education, organizational level, and OD titles of its membership.

Kegan's results yield a profile of the OD practitioner that is reasonably generalizable to a majority of OD practitioners. He found three-quarters of the OD Network membership to be men, with close to 90 percent white. Interestingly, Kegan found that OD practitioners were similar in age, with an average age of 47. Further, he found that close to 75 percent of those responding were internal consultants. Of these, 44 percent were working in industry, 14 percent in education, 6 percent in government, and 5 percent in other types of organizations such as the military and health care.

Both internal and external consultants were similar concerning their time usage, with 44 percent of their work time devoted to an OD effort, much of this time in the role of a sole change agent. Of great interest was Kegan's finding that on the whole, OD practitioners were very satisfied with their work. In fact, those professionals holding dual responsibility see their OD work as less stressful than their principal job. Only a quarter of those responding reported that their work was stressful to any great extent. Of those responding, the average gross income was approximately $32,500, with half of the daily fees being charged in the $300–$500-a-day range.

Of specific interest was Kegan's finding concerning education of OD practitioners. Not surprisingly, most reported having had some form of specific OD training. In terms of formal training, 60 percent had a masters degree, 14 percent a baccalaureate degree, and 26 percent held doctorate degrees. However, only 70 percent had some form of certification or professional licensure. These findings are not at all surprising given the number of programs now offering OD, and OD specialities.

Today, several doctoral programs are offered in OD in schools such as Case Western Reserve and Brigham Young, with numerous masters degree programs available from schools such as Bowling Green and American University. However, the vast number of practitioners without formal education in OD obtain their training and background from attending workshops presented by NTL, University Associates, and the Gestalt Institute of Cleveland, etc, who provide a curriculum for OD certification. Lippitt and Lippitt (1978) note that "the training of consultants has been a haphazard process. Only recently, have workshops and courses for developing consultants' skills appeared" (p. 104).

Although educational programs have been growing in number, the overwhelming number of practitioners and theorists with formal education come from administrative and social sciences, where OD was provided as a subspecialty. Programs in Business Administration, Public Administration, Health Care Administration, Sociology, as well as Clinical, Social, Community, and Industrial/Organizational Psychology have all produced large numbers of practitioners and theorists who practice OD, either full or part-time. Drawing from this heterogeneous pool of people has shaped the past, present, and the future of OD through interdisciplinary values, orientations, and approaches.

How the education and skills should be acquired has been, and will continue to be the subject of divisive debate within the field. A significant number of scholars are advocates of a formal interdisciplinary education. Yet others argue that some of the more effective change agents come from line management, without the benefit of formal OD training. However, a growing number of practitioners and scholars are advocates of a combination of a formal education that is interdisciplinary in nature, and an experiential education involving supervised application of theory and techniques. Noting this problem, Havelock (1973) states:

Most of the tactics or functions discussed (or interventions) cannot simply be picked up casually from a manual. They are skills which have to be learned. A good tactic badly executed may be worse than no tactic at all. (p. 153)

Over the past two decades, a significant amount of research has been produced concerning the stages of careers and general career development of organizational participants (Schein, 1978; and Hall, 1976). Very little is known however with respect to the careers of OD professionals. There are two reasons for this lack of knowledge. First, the field is difficult to conceptualize because of the interdisciplinary background and application of the field of study, the newness of the field notwithstanding. Second, the problem is compounded by boundary spanning and marginality that OD practitioners engage in. That is, there are many internal or external OD practitioners, and the differentiation between them is often quite difficult. Moreover, many practicing change agents practice OD only part of the time, and therefore have dual careers such as managers, teachers, professors, ministers, and social workers.

One attempt to conceptualize the career process in OD has been the work by Cotton and Browne (1978). Figure 2.1 illustrates their conceptualization of a systems model of OD careers. Shown are primary occupational subsystems involved in OD (professor and external OD professional, external OD professional, and internal OD professional), the transition point between them, as well as career decisions and various role alternatives. A basic aspect of Figure 2.1 is that career paths for internal or external OD practitioners, who are academically trained or not, can be illustrated.

As shown, career paths into three employment categories come from the pool of graduates from the university, as well as from managers and staff of the organization. Also shown are the points of transition between these categories. Of specific interest however is Cotton and Browne's notion of career burnout after entry into and adoption of one of the roles in OD. Based on Mitchell's (1977) notion of career burnout, and Herzberg's (1968) notion of work motivation, Figure 2.1 demonstrates the progression of consultant burnout and eventual career dropout. According to Cotton and Browne (1978), this burnout occurs when the consultant becomes experienced in OD or has spent a great deal of time in the OD field. This progression is influenced and moderated by the change roles one adopts.

Career burnout can be caused by hygiene factors (supervision, policies, work conditions, interpersonal relations) or lack thereof, as well as the absence or presence of motivational factors such as, responsibility, growth, quality of supervision, or work itself. As a result of career burnout, several different kinds of career choices are

FIG. 2.1. A Systems Model of Organizational Development Careers

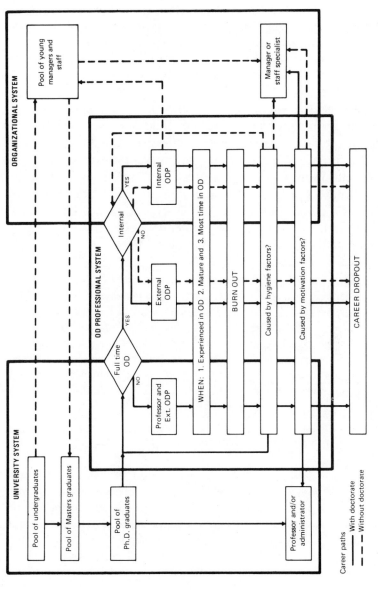

Source: From Cotton, C. C. and Brown, P. J. "A Systems Model of Organizational Development Careers," *Group and Organizational Studies* 3, no. 2, 1978, p. 187.

35

available by adopting a different role, or leaving OD entirely. Cotton and Browne state:

> Recurring burnout will result as hygiene problems drive the OD practitioner to seek yet another and, it is hoped, less punishing setting in which to practice OD. At this point, experienced internal OD practitioners without doctorates will sometimes become external OD practitioners if they have attained sufficient experience and visibility. Others will move to an internal OD job in another organization or into a non-OD staff role. Those with doctorates have, of course, the same full range of choices they had upon initial entry. (p. 192)

Regardless of where and how the OD consultant gains his/her education, training, or experience, distinguished scholars and practitioners in the OD field have given extensive thought to the qualities necessary for becoming a competent interventionist (Albrecht, 1982; Lippitt and Lippitt, 1978; Havelock 1972; Warrick and Donovan, 1979; Varney, 1980; Zaltman and Duncan, 1977; Rogers and Shoemaker, 1971; and Lippitt, 1982). Noting a variety of educational problems and professional development issues involved in developing OD competencies, Varney (1980) notes that

> The danger to the field in not defining an approach to professional development is obvious. Ill-trained practitioners increase the susceptibility of charlatanism and a quick treatment of organizational problems. This can cost us and the client a considerable amount of credibility within our own ranks as well as with other professional groups and organizations. People practicing in the field of OD should face up to the need to define a broad development framework. Such a framework need not eliminate innovation but should enhance individual development while preserving the uniqueness of the field. (p. 31)

Similarly, Lippitt (1982) states that

> There is much evidence to indicate that most of management disenchantment with past renewal efforts has been created by persons who turn knobs and pull levers without adequate understanding of the forces and factors they are trying to influence. The professional renewal facilitators of the future—no matter what they may be called—should be specialists of broad comprehension and ability, rather than book-learned manipulators of methods. (p. 371)

OD Skills and Competencies

The route to becoming an OD consultant is by no means a restrictive one. Indeed the OD field is a unique one in the respect that its members come from many different backgrounds and training. As previously noted, only in recent years have curricula been developed for education in the OD field, per se. Even with the advent of formal education programs, the overwhelming majority of available OD consultants do not hold specific degrees in the field of OD. They instead come from widely divergent formal educational tracks. While there may be problems associated with this educational variance, it does add to the intellectual richness of the profession generally, and to OD technology specifically.

While education is important, the "seasoning" necessary for successful OD interventions can only partially be learned in a classroom setting (Warrick and Donovan, 1979). On-the-job experience is a must for accelerating the seasoning process. Naismith (1971), noting this problem, divides the means of acquiring needed change-agent characteristics (skills, knowledge, attitudes) into formal education and informal learning experience. Aspects of formal education include literature of the behavioral sciences and organizations, tutorial under an experienced practitioner, individual therapy and sensitivity training, training labs, and university courses in OD. Means of acquiring informal learning experience include exposure to organizations, discussion with peers, and experimentation.

Having analyzed these various skills and competencies, Albrecht (1982) developed four major skill categories that present OD practitioners need and that future OD efforts will require.

The first of these categories is skill of influence, which is defined as the ability to access the organizational power structure. Generally, this category would involve an understanding of marketing principles or the ability to sell oneself through the complex behaviors required to achieve that end.

The second skill category enumerated by Albrecht is termed analytical skills. The attending behaviors could be comfortably lumped into what could be termed organizational analysis and diagnosis. The medium through which these skill needs are satisfied would be a thorough grounding in the instrumentation available for organizational diagnostic activities, a sound understanding of research design and statistics, and a necessary comfortableness with computer technology.

The third skill category is synthesizing skills. The behaviors required here are not limited to the synthesis of data. Required behaviors include homogenizing data with organizational realities, e.g., varying ideas, interests, goals, participant skills, and organizational needs.

Implementation skills round out the needed skills for OD interventionists. According to Albrecht, the skills used here center on the notion of making the new programs and approaches operational. A major required quality needed by the change agent is the ability to motivate the organizational participants to effect the new approaches by altering and redesigning where necessary.

Menzel (1975) developed a list of change-agent skills into a comprehensive taxonomy. He delineated the roles of a change agent, the phases of change, and related each to 25 specific OD skills. Using the roles of educating, diagnosing, consulting, and linking, and the stages of unfreezing, movement, and refreezing, Menzel's taxonomy is especially helpful in investigating the overlap of various skills required for specific change roles and specific stages of change. According to Menzel, in each of the assumed roles, various skills are required depending upon which phase of the change process is in operation. For example, in the role of an educator the change agent may need to use teaching skills in order to establish a change relationship during the unfreezing phase of the OD effort. In the role of a diagnostician, the change agent might have to call upon skills in instrument/survey design for generalization and stabilization during the refreezing period, as well as diagnosis of problems in the unfreezing and movement stages. Similarly, the skill of resource linker is a skill which is functional and relevant at every stage of change.

Havelock (1972), in an attempt to develop educational curricula for change agents, established three areas of mastery for change agents. Table 2.1 illustrates the theories change agents should know and the skills change agents should possess. In all, Havelock enumerated 35 different areas of mastery under the respective categories. Havelock notes that his master list is by no means exhaustive and is too general to constitute behaviorally specific outcomes. Havelock's work is important, however, in that it was one of the first attempts to differentiate needed areas of skill and knowledge or values and personal attributes of change agents.

TABLE 2.1. Educational Curriculum for Change Agents

1. The change agent should have these attitudes and values:
   Primary concern for benefit of the ultimate user (usually students and communities in the case of education).
   Primary concern for benefit of society as a whole.
   Respect for strongly-held values of others.
   Belief that change should provide the greatest good to the greatest number.
   Belief that changees have a need and a right to understand why changes are being made (rationale) and to participate in choosing among alternative change means and ends.
   A strong sense of his own identity and his own power to help others.
   A strong concern for helping without hurting, for helping with minimum jeopardy to the long or short term well-being of society as a whole and/or specific individuals within it.
   Respect for existing institutions as legitimate barriers unless or until the change agent has gained a clear understanding of why such institutions are there and how they can be replaced without serious cost to the human systems to which they pertain.

2. The change agent should know these things:
   That individuals, groups, and societies are open interrelating systems.
   How his role fits into a larger social context of change.
   Alternative conceptions of his own role now and his potential role in the future.
   How others will see his role.
   The range of human needs, their interrelationships and probable priority ranking at different stages in the life cycle.
   The resource universe and the means of access to it.
   The value bases of different subsystems in the macrosystem of education.
   The motivational bases of different subsystems in the macrosystem.
   Why people and systems change and resist change.
   How people and systems change and resist change.
   The knowledge, attitudes and skills required of a change agent.
   The knowledge, attitudes and skills required of an effective user of resources.

3. The change agent should possess these skills:
   How to build and maintain change project relationships with others.
   How to bring people to a conception of their priority needs in relation to priority needs of others.
   How to resolve misunderstandings and conflicts.
   How to build value bridges.
   How to convey to others a feeling of power to bring about change.
   How to build collaborative teams for change.
   How to organize and execute successful change projects.
   How to convey to others the knowledge, values, and skills he possesses.
   How to bring people to a realization of their own resource-giving potential.
   How to expand people's openness to use of resources, internal and external.
   How to expand awareness of the resource universe.
   How to work collaboratively (synergistically) with other resource systems.
   How to relate effectively to powerful individuals and groups.
   How to relate effectively to individuals and groups who have a strong sense of powerlessness.
   How to make systemic diagnosis of client systems and how to generate self-diagnosis by clients.

Source: From Havelock, R. G. *Training for Change Agents*: A Guide to the Design of Training Programs in Education and Other Fields. Ann Arbor, Michigan: Center for Research on Utilization of Scientific Knowledge, Institute for Social Research, The University of Michigan, 1972, pp. 64–66.

Based on work developed by the Bureau of Technical Assistance at the Agency for International Development, Zaltman and Duncan (1977) have also elaborated on the basic qualifications, administrative qualifications, and interpersonal relations. Zaltman and Duncan further elaborate upon the change agent's job orientation which consists of motivation and drive, acceptance of constraints, and development of commitment. This elaboration of basic qualifications also includes emotional maturity and leadership. Emotional maturity consists of components of character and personal security. Leadership includes components of poise, backbone, and political finesse.

A study conducted by Warrick and Donovan (1979) sampled 20 well-known OD experts and 50 internal practitioners concerning the skills required to be a successful OD practitioner. This method enabled them to isolate 40 skills amenable to four categories: knowledge skills, consulting skills, conceptual skills, and human skills. Figure 2.2 shows the various skills associated with successful OD practice.

Knowledge skills include the behavioral sciences, business management, and training knowledge. Consulting skills include proposal preparation, report writing, organizational diagnostic skills, and an ability to develop sound relationships with the client. Conceptual skills include behaviors that allow the change agent to see the OD process as a system of interacting and influencing parts and to be able to view this complex system from an innovative and creative perspective. Human skills are inextricably linked to an introspective view of the change agent. The introspective components include the change agent's self concept, sensitivity and emotional balance, coupled with the capacity to model these characteristics. Warrick and Donovan note with tongue-in-cheek that the skills identified by their survey might be more fitting for a superwoman or superman rather than for OD practitioners.

Another study by Lippitt and Lippitt (1978) asked 32 practicing consultants for their ideas concerning consultant competencies. Results of the study revealed skills in three broad competency areas—knowledge areas, skill areas, and attitude areas.

Knowledge areas included such categories as grounding in the behavioral sciences, administrative philosophies, organizational systems, educational and training methodologies, developmental psychology, design of change processes, personality strengths and weaknesses, biases, as well as various value and philosophical systems.

FIG. 2.2. Survey of Organization Development Skills

KNOWLEDGE SKILLS	CONSULTING SKILLS	CONCEPTUAL SKILLS	HUMAN SKILLS
☐ Organization Development ☐ Organization Behavior (Individual, Group, Intergroup, and Whole Organization Behavior) ☐ Behavioral Sciences ☐ Management ☐ General Business (Accounting, Finance, Marketing, Management Information System, Budgeting, Etc.) ☐ Training Technology ☐ An Awareness of Current Developments in OD	☐ Proposal Writing ☐ Marketing Programs & Ideas ☐ Diagnosing Organizations ☐ Synthesizing Data ☐ Report Writing ☐ Problem Solving ☐ Team Building ☐ Conflict Resolution ☐ Process Consultation ☐ Training & Development Skills ☐ An Ability to Identify & Respond to an Organization's Real Needs ☐ An Ability to Quickly Adapt to Changing Situations ☐ An Ability to Quickly Establish Client Trust & Rapport ☐ An Ability to Obtain Lasting Results	☐ A Sound Philosophical Base Concerning Human Behavior, Management, Organization Behavior, Learning Behavior, and Organization Development ☐ A Systems View of Organizations and the Environments in Which They Operate ☐ An Ability to Visualize, Design, and Manage Long-Range Programs, Training, Interventions, and Follow-up Programs ☐ An Ability to Understand and Communicate Theories, Principles, Models, and Ideas ☐ An Ability to Innovate	☐ A Genuine Caring for People ☐ A Positive Attitude ☐ Self-Awareness ☐ Self-Discipline ☐ Good Rational/ Emotional Balance ☐ Integrity ☐ Helping Skills (Understanding, Empathetic, Good Listener and Coach, Good at Checking Out Perceptions, Assertive, Good at Giving and Receiving Feedback) ☐ Sensitivity to Organizational Needs ☐ Leveling & Confronting Skills ☐ Persuasiveness & Persistence ☐ A Willingness to Take Risks ☐ An Ability to Successfully Handle Stress & Frustration ☐ A Good Sense of Humor ☐ An Ability to Model & Practice Healthy Behavior

OD SKILLS EVALUATION

Evaluate yourself on each of the OD skills by placing the appropriate answer in each box. Total your scores and divide by two and compare the result below.

1 = Poor	2 = Below Average	3 = Average	4 = Good	5 = Excellent
Excellent 90-100	Good 80-89	Average 70-79	Below Average 60-69	Poor Below 60

Source: From Warwick, D. D. and Donovan, T. "Surveying O.D. Skills." *Training and Development Journal* 33, no. 9, 1979, p. 23.

Lippitt and Lippitt's research also identified a vast number of skill areas. Among these were communication skills, teaching and persuasion skills, counseling skills, ability to build and form relationships, sensitivity, and planning and implementing skills. Included in this list would be skills in utilization of intervention methods, skill in designing surveys and data collection methods, ability to diagnose problems, ability to be flexible, and problem solving skills. Additional areas included the attitude of professional maturity, open-mindedness, and possession of a humanistic value system.

More recently Lippitt (1982) outlined and refined previous work performed in conjunction with Nadler (1967). Lippitt maintains that modern change agents should be professionally prepared in four roles. These are as a planning leader, an information and communications link, a learning specialist, and as a problem solver with management. In the role of a planning leader, a change agent should be an able program administrator with a knowledge of management principles and concepts. As a communications link the change agent should be capable of bringing together divergent organizational entities in a comprehendable fashion that will allow maximum fusion of inputs. As a learning specialist, the change agent must know fundamentals of learning and education both at the cognitive and affective level. As a problem solver with management, the facilitator should act as a resource to management in the solution of organizational problems. Finally, the change agents should have the skills to assist management from their perspective through the entire change effort.

Research by Carey and Varney (1983) collected data from over 600 randomly selected members of the OD Division of the American Society of Training and Development. Respondents were asked to rate their perception of the classification and relative importance of specific OD skills, and which skills contribute to the success of three common intervention types. Of the 62 specific skills analyzed, the ones most crucial to success were interpersonal skills, perception skills, ability to deal with resistance, ability to encourage participation, ability to see different perspectives, ability to confront, ability to assess leadership climate/cohesion, ability to create an open atmosphere, ability to manage conflict, ability to be clear, and the ability to use data.

A Social Ecological Approach to Development

While there are obvious differences in the articulation styles of experts such as Lippitt (1982). Menzel (1975), Warrick and Donovan

(1979), Havelock (1972), and Zaltman and Duncan (1977), etc., there is general agreement concerning required skill areas for OD consultants. Unfortunately, much less is known about an appropriate methodology to analyze and develop change agent skills and competencies. This is due to two reasons. First, relatively little is known about the development of complex human skills required of a change agent. Second, change-agent skills or competencies are comprised of many aspects of human behavior. That is, behavioral attributes, interpersonal attributes, and cognitive attributes are often required simultaneously for the successful application of a change agent's skills.

For the OD practitioner, what are cognitive, behavior, and interpersonal skills? There is still much debate within contemporary psychology regarding the finite distinction between cognitive, behavioral and interpersonal human skills. There are, however, certain common elements or factors, from which cognitive, behavioral, and interpersonal skills can be distinguished. From a social ecological perspective of human skill development proposed earlier (Wooten and White, 1980), consultant skills, irrespective of nature or complexity, comprise the following four elements:

1. The use of some attribute or factor of the individual (change agent).
2. The application of some attributes or factor to a practical purpose or situation (an organization).
3. The utilization of an attribute or factor of the individual that can be demonstrated by performance (an intervention).
4. The skill can be improved by practice (change-agent experience).

If OD consultancy skills are comprised of these four elements, the notion that there are specific cognitive, behavioral, and interpersonal skills is congruent with the ideas of Menzel (1975), Lippitt (1982), and Havelock (1972).

Cognitive factors can be defined as the intellectual and judgmental aspects of the individual or change agent. Cognitive factors or attributes are those that are specific or unique to the individual alone and deal with mental operations and processes. Such factors include various aptitudes, learning ability, various perceptual abilities, relative intelligence or general knowledge, decision-making and problem-solving ability, memory, abstraction, search strategies, insight, coding capacity, and hypothesis testing, to name a few. These are similar to and would be subsumed under the "intellectual abilities" delineated by Lippitt (1982) and Lippitt and Lippitt (1978). Warrick and Donovan (1978) refer to these traits as knowledge, consulting and conceptual skills, while Havelock (1972) refers to them as attitudes and values and skills that change agents should possess. These relate in part to what Albrecht (1982) defines as analytical and synthesizing skills.

Relevant to change agents, behavioral factors can be defined as the emotional and attitudinal aspects of the individual. Behavioral factors or attributes are those that are specific or unique to the individual or change agent alone and deal with the individual's personality operations and processes. Such factors include ego states, self-concept, motivation, frustration, avoidance, sociability, prejudice, tolerance, confidence, independence, sensitivity, conformity, passivity, competitiveness, conventionality, trust, acceptance, dominance, extroversion, rigidity, apathy, defensiveness, and conservatism. Behavioral factors relate directly to Havelock's (1972) notion of attitudes and values change agents should possess, as well as Zaltman and Duncan's (1977) discussion of a change agent's emotional maturity. Warrick and Donovan (1979) and Lippitt and Lippitt (1978) see behavioral factors as human skills and attitudes.

Interpersonal factors can be defined as the application of cognitive and behavioral factors of the individual to situations involving other individuals. Interpersonal factors or attributes are those factors that are specific or unique to the individual alone and deal with the processes and operations of two or more individuals experiencing the same environment or common situation. Such factors may include the ability to build acceptance, the ability to reduce conflict and aggression, the ability to provide empathy and understanding, to facilitate decisions, to reduce prejudice, to motivate, to learn from others and facilitate learning from others, and the ability to reduce anxiety.

A change agent's ability, via interpersonal factors, to operate effectively in the interpersonal world are essential to "consulting and linking" processes (Menzel, 1975), and implementation of new operations and procedures (Lippitt, 1982). These interpersonal skills relate directly to Lippitt and Lippitt's (1978) area of "skills". Skills include the ability to communicate, to counsel others, form relationships, and to have sensitivity. Albrecht's (1982) refers to interpersonal factors as influencing skills.

Although these definitions do distinguish between cognitive, be-havioral, and interpersonal factors, relevant to change-agent skills, they in no way reflect the possible inclusion or exclusion of many others. It can be argued that these factors and their combination can become skills and competencies relevant to OD by use, application to a practical situation or purpose, demonstration by performance, and improvement by practice over time. Consultant skills, like all human skills, are therefore complex phenomenon, and are difficult to con-ceptualize and measure.

Figure 2.3 demonstrates the complexity of human and change-agent skills. The CBID model proposes that cognitive factors, behav-ioral factors, and interpersonal factors, produce some form of overt result and subsequent success or failure of that result. Here the cogni-tive and behavioral factors are those that are specific or unique to the change agent, while interpersonal factors involve the change agent's application of cognitive and behavioral factors to an OD situation.

FIG. 2.3. The C.B.I.D. Learning Model

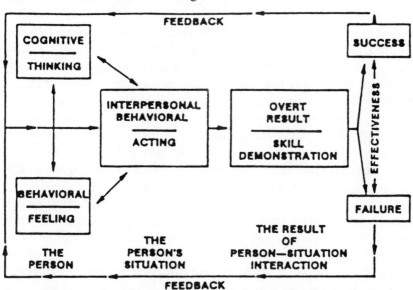

Source: From Wooten, K. C. and White, L. P. C.B.I.D.: Cognitive, Behav-ioral, and Interpersonal Development–A Social Learning Approach to Skill De-velopment. *Journal of Experiential Learning and Simulation* 2, no. 3, 1980, p. 92.

The arrows between the cognitive, behavioral, and interpersonal factors indicate an interaction or dependency between them. The consultant's cognitive factors are therefore greatly dependent upon the behavioral factors, as well as the organizational environment or situation encountered. Similarly, behavioral factors are greatly dependent upon cognitive factors, as well as the organizational environment or the situation encountered. Furthermore, interpersonal factors of change agents are dependent upon their cognitive and behavioral factors.

The result of the application of cognitive and behavioral factors to the client system is some form of "overt result." The overt result is directly observable and measurable and is demonstrated by the "performance" of the change agent. This is a function of the consultant-organizational situation interaction or combination. The result then will be seen as a success or failure, depending upon its effectiveness. The relative effectiveness, or the success or failure of this overt result, acts as "feedback" to the change agent and can start the intervention scenario over again.

Figure 2.3 also illustrates that cognitive factors can be seen as thinking. The behavioral factors can be seen as feeling while interpersonal factors can be seen as acting. Thus, the three essential factors are thinking (cognitive), feeling (behavioral), and acting (interpersonal). Figure 2.3 illustrates that what a change agent thinks (knows, remembers, conceives, etc.) is dependent upon how he/she feels (attitude, personality, motivation, etc.) and how they act in the organizational situation encountered (the ability to be accepted, ability to facilitate decisions, ability to reduce anxiety, etc.). On the other hand, what change agents feel is most certainly dependent upon what they think and how they act in any given situation. Obviously, how a change agent acts in a given intervention or client system interaction is dependent upon what they think and how they feel.

The premise of the CBID model is the conceptualization of human behavior referred to as interactionism. Interactionism is the ecologically oriented inquiry of human behavior by prominent contemporay psychologists such as Ekehammar (1974), and Bowers (1973). The basic tenet of interactionism is that neither the situation nor the person as single entities is emphasized. It is the interaction of the two that receives focus. The use of this interaction concept provides a vehicle for an analysis of the synergism inherent in the process of OD.

The transformation that takes place during an OD intervention requires skill and knowledge in numerous and wide-ranging areas. The work of Lippitt (1982), Lippitt and Nadler (1967), Warrick and Donovan (1979), Albrecht (1982), and Menzel (1975), illustrates this diversity of OD consulting requirements. An alternative approach might be to view OD skills as the application of knowledge and behavioral factors or to practice what is known and felt. Since much of what an OD practitioner does is process oriented, or the application of knowledge, the interventionist becomes an intricate part of an OD effort. This kind of involvement in the development effort greatly enhances the probability of success and requires cognitive, behavioral, and interpersonal competence.

Table 2.2 is a listing of generally accepted requisite skill areas for OD as they relate to the cognitive, behavioral, and interpersonal aspects of OD consultancy.

TABLE 2.2. OD Consultant Competencies

COGNITIVE	BEHAVIORAL	INTERPERSONAL
Group Dynamics	Risk Taker	Model
Business Function (Accounting, Finance)	Self-Awareness	Leveling & Confronting
Individual Behaviors	Self-Discipline	Ability to Handle Stress
Training	Sensitivity	Ability to Gain Trust & Rapport
Diagnosis & Analysis	Caring	
Organizational Communication	Integrity	
	Values	

Shown first under the cognitive factors necessary for an effective change agent is an understanding of group dynamics. An effective change agent must have an understanding of group processes at the intragroup and intergroup level and how these function in the formal as well as the informal organization. A knowledge of business operations is also necessary for a change agent. For example, while it may be unlikely that a given change agent has in-depth knowledge of business technology, he should be familiar with the impact of budgetary constraints as they affect organizational processes and the OD effort itself.

Since organizations comprise human interactions a competent change agent should have knowledge of human behavior. He should understand the ways in which personality, intelligence, values, and emotions of organizational participants influence the OD process. Without this knowledge a change agent cannot conceptualize, plan, nor induce organizational change.

Knowledge of diagnosis and analysis techniques and training are of prime importance to a change agent (Havelock and Havelock, 1973). Diagnosis of organizational processes and behaviors requires that the change agent be comfortable with various data-gathering techniques and instrumentation. Once data are gathered they must be analyzed and reported back to the organization in comprehendable form. This process can be fruitful to the extent that a change agent is comfortable with statistical analysis and data processing systems.

The last of the cognitive elements is organizational communications. As organizations undergo the OD process and begin to be a part of the change effort, major changes are implicit in the technology of the organizational communication system. Technological and structural changes produce changes in both the formal and informal organizational communication system, that can impact directly upon the change effort.

Definitionally, behavioral components refer to the emotional and attitudinal characteristics of the change agent. In order to achieve success in OD, knowledge of oneself is essential. The change agent must be aware of his value structure and its role in the OD process. Given the sensitive nature of organizational and personal data, an interventionist must have impeccable integrity and personal characteristics. If these "feeling" aspects of a change agent's repertoire are not refined, the caring and sensitivity of the change agent are significantly impaired.

Interpersonal factors involve the application of the cognitive and behavioral components to bring about the change effort. Activities such as modeling, leveling and confronting, the ability to handle stress in oneself as well as in others, and the ability to gain trust and develop rapport with the change target are shown in Table 2.2. To accomplish these change processes the change agent must be able to gain acceptance, to facilitate decision making, to learn from others and reduce anxieties about the change effort.

This social-ecological view of skill requirements for the OD interventionist brings to light some conclusions. The cognitive components for change agents are generally provided for. Degree programs at colleges and universities fulfill these needs adequately. Courses in business, computer science, statistics, industrial psychology, as well as other needed cognitive components are available. However, opportunities for behavioral and interpersonal development are significantly more scarce. Institutions such as NTL and University Associates meet these needs to an extent, but only on a personal demand basis. The OD industry will gain significant momentum toward becoming a profession providing that learning institutions (colleges and universities, OD professional organizations) establish the means whereby these aspects of change-agent behavior (feeling and action) are analyzed and dealt with on the same level as cognitive factors. This kind of symmetry is necessary for the maximum derivable benefits of an OD effort, whether the education and training of OD consultants adopts the CBID approach (Fig. 2.3) or Kolb's (1976) model of adult learning advocated by Lippitt (1982).

The well-rounded change agents to be produced, educational experiences must provide them the opportunity to observe and reflect from experience, develop theories and deductions, as well as provide new situations for the would-be change agent's concepts to be tested and proven.

VALUES OF THE PROFESSION

The Influence of Values on Theory and Practice

Human values have played a crucial role in the development of the OD profession. Without question, values of the profession have shaped the development of OD from its early beginnings. The issue of values rests at the very center of controversies involving professional ethics and practice. The two annual reviews of organizational development by Friedlander and Brown (1974) and Alderfer (1977), and texts by Margulies and Raia (1978), Huse (1980), and French and Bell (1976) illustrate OD's humanistic and democratic value orientation.

Friedlander and Brown's (1974) review of the literature indicates that OD's humanistic and democratic values are largely an extension of McGregor's (1960) Theory-Y assumption and Tannenbaum and

Davis's (1969) notion of the value transformation in society. Mc-Gregor based his theory on the contention that employees view work and effort as natural, that they can exercise self-direction and control, seek responsibility, and commit to objectives. Likewise, Tannenbaum and Davis's observation on value transformations in society places emphasis on viewing man as basically good and views him in a holistic fashion. Their value transformation aims toward organizationally relevant purposes rather than personal ones, toward more trusting and appropriate confrontation, toward risk taking and willingness to risk, and a greater emphasis on collaboration.

Alderfer's (1977) review of the literature parallels the work of Friedlander. Alderfer states "a strong force motivating the emergence of the field has been the desire to humanize organizations, that is, to enable organizations to be more responsible to the human concerns of members" (p. 198). This fundamental grounding in humanistic values is also articulated by Bennis (1969), Kahn (1974), Miles (1975), and by Golembiewski (1972). Alderfer's review also reflects OD's emphasis on organizational effectiveness. He observes that

> Along with the pursuit of humanistic values, OD has also been advocated as a set of technologies for improving organizational effectiveness of organizations. In the earliest days of OD, there was less reason to question whether these two classes of values conflicted with each other because the scope of OD application was much narrower than it is today. Although there were variations among OD theorists, and practitioners in terms of relative emphasis on these two classes of values, most people in the field believed that they could pursue both with minimal conflict. . . . Today, there is a substantial and significant debate about the value implications of much of OD work among thinkers in the field. (p. 198)

What then are the specific values of the OD profession that has given rise to this controversy? In their review of OD, Margulies and Raia (1978) have identified six specific values that the OD profession embraces. They are:

1. Providing opportunities for people to function as human beings rather than as resources in the productive process.
2. Providing opportunities for each organization member, as well as for the organization itself, to develop to his full potential.
3. Seeking to increase the effectiveness of the organization in terms of all of its goals.

4. Attempting to create an environment in which it is possible to find exciting and challenging work.
5. Providing opportunities for people in organizations to influence the way in which they relate to work, the organization, and the environment.
6. Treating each human being as a person with a complex set of needs, all of which are important in his work and in his life. (p. 137)

Based on earlier work by French (1969), French and Bell (1976) find that change agents subscribe to a comparable set of values. This set of values constitutes four primary beliefs on the part of applied behavior scientists. First is the belief that the need and aspirations of human beings are the reason for an organized effort in society. Therefore, values of change agents focus on the personal growth of people in organizations. Second, change agents believe that work and life can become more meaningful and organizational participation is a legitimate part of organizational culture. Third, change agents have a commitment, via action research, to improve the effectiveness of organizations. Fourth, applied behavioral scientists place a high value on the democratization of organizations through power equalization processes. These values of change agents are derived from assumptions underlying many OD interventions. (See Table 2.3.)

Similar to French and Bell's (1976) notion of OD values, Warrick and Thompson (1980) also analyzed the values characterizing the OD field. The first value is that OD has a client centered approach. Second, OD is for the whole organization and should begin at the top. Third, an expert change agent must lead the OD effort. The fourth value is that openness and trust are needed to have a healthy and effective organization. Fifth, participative management and power equalization are valued. Last, OD practitioners hold Theory-Y assumptions about people.

In perhaps the most critical investigation of OD values, Friedlander (1976) has explored OD's underlying values and their implications to OD. Based on Hainer's (1968) basic value philosophies, Friedlander discussed three value concepts which underly the OD profession. These three value concepts are rationalism, pragmatism, and existentialism. Friedlander argues that the balance of these three value concepts affect what change agents perceive as important and worthy.

Rationalists hold the value of the scientific method as being of primary importance. This value orientation focuses on logic and con-

TABLE 2.3. OD's Underlying Assumptions

Assumptions About Individuals
1. Most individuals desire personal growth and development when placed in an environment which is supportive and challenging.
2. Most individuals are capable of making a great contribution to their organization, but the organization often squelches this by not rewarding them or by penalizing them.

Assumptions About Group Members
1. The work group is extremely important in the development of satisfaction and feelings of competence.
2. Most people want to get along with their work group and be accepted by them.
3. Group members must help their formal leader in sharing leadership functions at all times.
4. Suppressing feelings of group members negatively affect their functioning. The climate of the group should be one of openness.
5. Interpersonal trust and support is lower in most groups than is desirable.

Assumptions About People In Organizational Systems
1. Most managers are members of overlapping work groups.
2. Changes in one subsystem of the organization will affect and be affected by other parts of the entire organization.
3. Resolving organizational conflict through win-lose strategies is not healthy for the organization's long term perspective.
4. When performance is increased by OD efforts, it needs to be supported and maintained by managerial changes in other subsystems of the organization.

Source: From French, W. L. and Bell, C. H. Jr. *Organizational Development*. Englewood Cliffs, N.J.: Prentice-Hall, 1973, pp. 66–70.

sistency; it relies on an empirical analytical base. It stresses OD techniques that are algorithmic in nature (i.e., a set of tried and true approaches with emphasis on control of the variables influencing the change process). Further, it holds that training techniques and methods be formulated on a sound empirical base with a concern for validity.

The second major value orientation, pragmatism, argues from a usefulness orientation. This approach would be concerned with the variance between pre- and postorganizational development measurements of organizational processes. Unfavorable variances would cause the change agent to discard the practice while a favorable variance would influence the change agent to retain the use of whatever techniques might have been employed. Experimentation is used to the extent of improving practice in that particular organizational milieu. The pragmatist value orientation is the embodiment of "action research" with a thrust toward practical knowledge and application. Whereas the rationalist approaches OD from a "why" vantage, the pragmatist has major concern with "how" as a point of origin.

The existential school of thought has its roots in the here and now experience. Rather than placing emphasis on changing the individual, the theme of the existentialist would be acceptance of that individual. Existentialism emphasizes the "is" or "being" configuration in the organizational world. Diagnosis assumes no special role in this value orientation, only in the sense of clarification of personal choices and the way in which that choice melds with organizational processes. Table 2.4 illustrates the contrast between the three value orientations.

Conner (1977) in his critical review of assumptions and values looked at the role of values in OD from a somewhat different point of view. He labels them rationality, trimodal humanism, elitism, and a clinical emphasis. Rationality bifurcates into scientific rationality and organizational rationality. Scientific rationality is congruent with the notions of Friedlander (1976) (i.e., a scientific approach, while organizational rationality refers to organizational effectiveness). Trimodal humanism refers first to human concerns; second, to the notion that collective behavior is the " . . . most efficacious means to both improved organizational performance and the goals of the humanism" (p. 637). The third form that trimodal humanism takes is that "such classic bureaucratic prescriptions as rigid hierarchy, centralization of authority, and highly formalistic rules and regulations are considered inconsistent with the humanistic goals of OD" (p. 637).

Conner's elitism is the third value orientation. The elitist approach stresses changing organizational participants when evidence suggests that much of the organizational change effort tends to focus on top management. Connor notes that this elitist approach, which is most frequently aimed at the managerial ranks, does not address the total organization. The fourth value position in OD according to Conner,

TABLE 2.4. Value = Concepts Relevant to Organizational Development

	Rationalism	Pragmatism	Existentialism
Purpose	to discover truth	to improve practice	to experience, choose, commit
Basic activity	think (knowledge-building)	do (acting)	exist (being)
Learning paradigm	conceptualize → define → manipulate ideas → conclusions	practice → experiment → valid feedback → improvement	experience → perceive → be aware → choose → commitment
Terms are	precisely defined	tentatively defined	need not be defined
Meaning emerges from	definition (concepts)	practice (results-consensus)	experience (perception)
Ingredients for learning	concepts, assumptions, logic, consistency	practice, experiment, feedback	awareness and confrontation of one's existence
Locus of Knowledge	the conceptual model	the organization practice	the individual experience
Reality is	objectivity and truth	workability and practice (validity)	subjective perception
Causes of good communication	semantic precision	consensual listening and understanding	shared feeling and resonance

Source: From Friedlander, F. *Purpose and Values in OD: Toward Personal Theory and Practice.* Madison, Wis.: Organizational Development Division, American Society For Training and Development, 1976, p. 18.

is that OD is strongly characterized by a clinical emphasis. He notes that "therapy is not just incidental, for many OD practitioners its the focal thrust of the activity" (p. 638).

Values and OD Practice

Whether values are classified along the lines advocated by Friedlander (1976) (i.e., rationalism, pragmatism, or existentialism) or from the point of view posited by Conner (1977) (i.e., rationalism, trimodal humanism, or elitism), the effects of these value orientations play a major role in the development and conduct of OD as a profession. Values can be seen to affect the practice of OD in two significant ways. First, values of the OD profession manifest themselves in the practice of change. Second, values inherent in OD are quite often conflicting.

Evidence is available that the value orientation of change agents has a significant impact on the choice of behavior in the OD profession. Investigating the relationship between values, cognitions, and actions of change agents, Tichy (1974), obtained data about the values of change agents, about how they conceptualized change, the techniques they used to carry out change, their personal characteristics, and their description of their work. The results of his investigation allowed for the development of a framework for studying the change agent and the change agent's role. Shown in Figure 2.4 is Tichy's model.

As illustrated there are five basic characteristics to the model. The first component is background characteristics, which include the change agent's education, age, religion, sex, etc. The second component is the change agent's evaluative component. That is, his attitudes toward social change, his aim in social change goals, and goals he feels that change agents should have (i.e., improved satisfaction of members, power equalization, etc.). This component, according to Tichy, represents the behavior of a change agent.

The third component shown in Figure 2.4 is the cognitive component, which refers to the change agent's concept about means of affecting changes. Concepts such as training, survey feedback, and t-groups are representative. The fourth component is change technology. Change technology refers to the skills the change agent uses, as well as the tools of change. The last component is concurrent

FIG. 2.4. The Change Agent's Framework

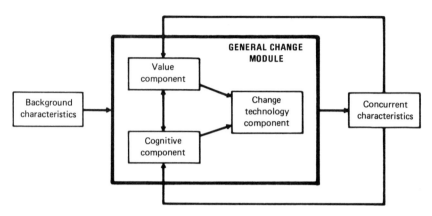

Source: From Tichy, N. M. "Agents of Planned Social Change: Congruence of Values, Cognitions and Actions." *Administrative Science Quarterly* 19, no. 2, 1974, p. 165.

characteristics. This refers to the actual behavior of the change agent. Thus, the basic premise of the model is the interdependency of the five components. According to Tichy, the model assumes that stress occurs in the change agent "when the value component and concurrent characteristics (the change agent's action) or the cognitive component and actions are not congruent" (p. 165).

In general, results of Tichy's investigation support the model. Based on the differences between the five components, Tichy identified four different types of change agents. These are: (1) outside pressure (OP); (2) organizational development (OD); (3) people change technology (PCT); and (4) analysis for the top (AFT). Outside pressure change agents are change advocates outside the organization such as civil rights leaders, and consumer advocates. Analysis for the top are those who rely primarily on operation research, systems analysis. OD change agents are those who work with problem-solving capabilities of the organization and other efforts to improve the social processes within the organization. People change technology are agents who work to change the way employees behave in such areas as job satisfaction, interest, and productivity.

Tichy found significant differences in the practical orientations of the four types of agents, as well as in their goals. Tichy notes the following:

Not surprisingly, the O.P.'s with the most extreme political orientation were the most critical in their view of society and the greatest advocates of radical change. The AFT's were the least critical and the least radical, and the OD's and PCT's were medium. (p. 171)

Concerning their values with respect to goal orientation he states:

The OP's were the most consistent, a not surprising finding, given the social and political idealism that motivate OP's and whose work is primarily directed to what "should be" in contrast to those who are more or less technicians for hire. A large percentage (80) of OD's were inconsistent, and although espousing with PCT's such goals as "democratic participation and solving social problems" their reports of what they actually did indicated that many were working to make systems more efficient and productive. A larger portion of PCT's than OD's reported that what they actually did was consistent with their goals. This was also true of AFT's. (p. 172)

Tichy found congruence between the five components, but that this congruence was moderated to a degree by change-agent type. According to Tichy all four types tend to have a high degree of congruence between the five components. However, all but the OP's included some inconsistencies. Most of the inconsistencies appeared in the relationship between interaction and cooperation. Thus, for the most part, value congruence or incongruence plays a major role in change-agent behavior. Of extreme significance however, was the finding that specific techniques used by the various change-agent types are a result of these components, or the value action/change techniques relationship. This relationship is illustrated in Table 2.5. Shown is a summary (OP's excluded) of the percentage of change-agent tactics used by the three major change-agent types. Just as dramatically then, values of change agents are directly linked to the techniques they used and the resultant behavior of the practitioner.

Related to Tichy's research is Friedlander's (1976) notion that choices for change agent behavior are a result of their particular value orientation (i.e., existentialism, pragmatism, rationalism).

The existentialist value orientation calls for the change agent to adopt the role of the "accepter of experience." A "change agent" role results from the pragmatist value orientation, while "the conceptual teacher-learner" role results from a rationalist value orientation. Each of these value orientations, therefore, calls for a different set of behaviors from the interventionist.

TABLE 2.5. Percentage of Different Change Tactics Used by
Change Agents

Change tactic	People-change technology (PCT)	Analysis-from-the-top (AFT)	Organization development (OD)
Confrontation meetings	47	39	95
Survey feedback	46	38	50
Job training	65	75	22
Sensitivity training	41	21	79
Team development	65	31	100
Technological innovation	71	89	63
Change in reward structure	82	71	58
Change in decision-making structure	76	96	94
Role clarification	100	95	100

Source: From Hellriegel, D. and Slocum, J. W. Jr. *Organizational Behavior*. St. Paul: West, 1979, p. 566.

Warrick and Thompson (1980) in their investigation of contemporary OD values and practice note the difference between the stated values of OD practitioners, their practicality or universal truths, and how they are applied. They state:

> We do believe that it is time to add some maturity to our practice of OD, to reevaluate some of our traditional OD value and practices, to reduce the discrepancies between theory and practice and to temper our OD value and practice with reality, practicality, and a theory base.

The checklist in Figure 2.5 is suggested to evaluate one's OD roles and practice, as well as the amount of congruence between values and practice.

Value orientation, then, plays a major role in OD theory and practice. What then is the role of value discrepancies in specific value dilemmas? Alderfer (1977), Friedlander (1976a and b) and Bowen (1977) have investigated value dilemmas facing the change agent.

FIG. 2.5. OD Practitioner Checklist

A CHECKLIST FOR BUILDING A THEORY OF PRACTICE

VALUES	PRACTICES
1. Are the values I am advocating realistic and appropriate to this organization?	1. Have I identified who the real client is by considering "all" persons or groups who could significantly influence this effort?
2. Have I discussed these values with the client to see if they meet the client's needs?	2. Have I adequately evaluated internal resources and what has been done in the past before recommending an approach to take?
3. If I am not using a whole organization, top to bottom approach, have I checked to see if change is realistic and likely to be accepted?	3. Have I done a thorough job of involving the client in the intervention design and in doing the necessary planning and commitment building?
4. Is my approach truly client-centered and tailored to the needs of this client?	4. Does my theory of practice provide me with guidelines for approaching the effort?
5. Who is the real change agent and what is my most productive role as a consultant?	5. Do I practice what I espouse in relating to the client, in modeling what I teach, and in my ethical practices?
6. Are my assumptions about people and organizations realistic and accurate? Do I continually test these assumptions?	6. Have I been able to maintain a high level of objectivity and confidentiality with this client's data?
7. Is participative management appropriate for this organization or for different parts of this organization?	7. Am I practicing OD as an ongoing process or as an event with a beginning and an end? How will I know when my relationship with the client is completed?
8. What degree of openness and trust is appropriate for this organization?	8. Have I considered the real cause of any resistance to change? Is the resistance legitimate? Could the program design or my style be the real cause?
9. Is change necessary or appropriate? Is the timing right?	9. What process do I have for structuring my relationship with my client?
10. Am I willing to continually test my theory of practice and accept the results as a way of building a more effective theory?	10. Am I able to be objective and yet realistic about data and how close it matches reality?
	11. Am I sensitive to the needs and feelings of my clients as they experience the OD effort?
	12. What am I doing to help the client reinforce the changes made in the organization?

Source: From Warrick, D. D. and Thompson, J. T. "Still Crazy After All These Years." *Training and Development Journal*, April, 1980, p. 19.

Friedlander and Brown (1974) and Alderfer (1977) maintain that much of the value debate is a result of the values themselves. That is, the discrepancy between the humanistic and democratic values, and the value of productivity and efficiency. The dilemmas here result from the efforts that require both value orientations to operate simultaneously. Concerning these situations, Bowen (1977) defines a value dilemma as "any situation where there is internal conflict between the values or needs of different members of a consulting team or where the consultants values are inconsistent with those of others involved in the consultation" (p. 544).

Concerning these various value dilemmas, Alderfer (1977) finds that the crux of value dilemmas rests in the notion and the use of power. He states:

> At the crux of the value disputes within OD is the problem of power. OD professionals must struggle with whether their professional competence (power) is being used to advance humane values and with whether they can harness enough power to bring about desirable change in human organization. (p. 199)

This value dilemma can be equally perplexing when the end result of assisting an organization may not be in the best interest of society. According to Friedlander (1976a) there are two basic dilemmas for the OD practitioners. The first deals with various roles to adopt as a result of ones value orientation. Second, is the OD professional's use and perspective of time. Friedlander states that with respect to roles to be adopted that

> A basic dilemma for the OD professional is whether to foster the individual self-acceptance and help him clarify his experience and choices (existentialist); Whether to become the subtle protagonist by suggesting or designing new experiences for the individual so he will emphasize (pragmatist), or whether to portray and gather knowledge for building more ideal models (rationalist). (p. 20)

SUMMARY

It can be seen that OD professionals and OD careers, while relatively under-researched can be characterized. OD professionals come from many disciplines and backgrounds, adding greatly to OD's heterogeneity in philosophy and practice. Using Cotton and Browne's (1978) model, practitioners can be seen to come from two basic sources: academic and line management, both of which result in various internal and external consultant roles. Although the method of acquisition is currently debatable, there is some agreement about the proper skills and abilities change agents require (Albrecht, 1982; Menzel, 1975; Havelock, 1972; Warrick and Donovan, 1979).

Through a social ecological approach, specific cognitive behavioral and interpersonal factors can be seen to be interdependent, resulting in clusters of consultant competencies required by change agents. Consultant competencies should include an understanding of group dynamics, a knowledge of business operation, a knowledge of human behavior, a knowledge of intervention and diagnostic technologies, a knowledge of organizational communication, appropriate value structure, and personal integrity.

Characteristics such as objectivity, the ability to confront, to handle stress, to gain trust, and to develop support, are equally important. A more balanced approach to change agent development is advocated, one that balances conceptual and analytical abilities with the ability for application and hypothesis testing in the field.

While there is general agreement about the skills required to be a competent change agent, there is likewise agreement about values for the OD profession and for the change agent. Values such as humanism, democracy, and power equalization are at the heart of theory and practice. These values, however, require a balance with concern for efficiency and productivity. Value concepts such as rationalism, pragmatism, and existentialism (Friedlander, 1976a and b), and rationality, trimodal humanism, elitism, and a dominant approach (Conner 1977) characterize the field. These values and value concepts influence the choice of change technologies by practitioners. Moreover, change agents can be characterized by their values and background characteristics (Tichy, 1974).

NOTES

Albrecht, K. *Organization Development: A Total Systems Approach to Positive Change in any Business Organization.* Englewood Cliffs, N.J.: Prentice-Hall, 1982.

Alderfer, C. P. "Organization Development." *Annual Review of Psychology* 28, 1977, 197–223.

Alderfer, C. P. and Berg, D. N. "Organization Development, The Profession and the Practitioner." In P.H. Mirvis and D. N. Berg (eds.), *Failures in Organizational Development and Change.* New York: Wiley-Interscience, 1977, 89–104.

Bennis, W. G. *Organization Development: Its Nature, Origins, and Prospects.* Reading, Mass.: Addison-Wesley, 1969.

Bowen, D. D. "Value Dilemmas in Organization Development." *Journal of Applied Behavioral Science* 13, no. 4, 1977, 543–56.

Bowers, K. S. "Situationalism in Psychology: An Analysis and Critique." *Psychological Review* 80, 1973, 307–336.

Carey, A. and Varney, G. H. "Which Skills Spell Success in OD?" *Training and Development Journal* 37, no. 4, 1983, 38–40.

Connor, P. E. "A Critical Inquiry into some Assumptions and Values Characterizing OD." *Academy of Management Review* 2, no. 4, 1977, 635–44.

Cotton, C. C. and Browne, P. J. "A Systems Model of Organization Development Careers." *Group and Organizational Studies* 3, no. 2, 1978, 185–98.

Ekehammar, B. "Interactionism in Personality From a Historical Perspective." *Psychological Bulletin* 81, 1974, 1026–49.

French, W. "Organization Development: Objectives, Assumptions, and Strategies." *California Management Review* 12, 1969, 23–24.

French, W. L. and Bell, C. H. Jr. *Organization Development.* 2d. ed. Englewood Cliffs, N.J.: Prentice-Hall, 1976.

Friedlander, F. *Purpose and Values in OD: Toward Personal Theory and Practice.* Madison, Wis.: American Society for Training and Development, 1976. *a*

Friedlander, F. "OD Reaches Adolescence: An Exploration of its Underlying Values." *Journal of Applied Behavioral Science* 12, no. 1, 1976, 7–12. *b*

Friedlander, F. and Brown, L. D. "Organization Development." *Annual Review of Psychology* 25, 1974, 313–41.

Golembiewski, R. T. *Renewing Organizations.* Itasca, Ill.: F. E. Peacock, Inc., 1972.

Hainer, R. M. "Rationalism, Pragmatism, and Existentialism: Perceived but Undiscovered Multicultural Problems." In E. Glatt and M. W. Shelly (eds.), *The Research Society.* New York: Gorron and Breach, 1968.

Hall, D. T. *Careers in Organizations.* Pacific Palisades, Cal.: Goodyear, 1976.

Havelock, R. G. *Training for Change Agents: A Guide to the Design of Training Programs in Education and Other Fields.* Ann Arbor: University of Michigan Press, 1972.

Havelock, R. G. *The Change Agents: Guide to Innovation in Education.* Englewood Cliffs, N.J.: Educational Technology Publications, 1973.

Havelock, R. G. and Havelock, M. C. *Training for Change Agents.* Ann Arbor: University of Michigan Press, 1973.

Hellriegel, D. and Slocum J. W. Jr. *Organizational Behavior*, 2d ed. St. Paul: West, 1979.

Herzberg, F. "One More Time: How Do You Motivate Employees?" *Harvard Business Review* 46, no. 1, 1968, 53-62.

Huse, E. F. *Organization Development and Change.* 2d ed. St. Paul: West, 1980.

Kahn, R. L. "Organization Development: Some Problems and Proposals." *Journal of Applied Behavioral Science* 10, 1974, 485-502.

Kegan, D. "A Profile of the OD Practitioner." *Group and Organizational Studies* 7, no. 1, 1982, 5-11.

Kolb, D. A. *Learning Style Inventory: Technical Manual.* Boston: McBer and Company, 1976.

Levinson, H. "The Clinical Psychologist as Organization Diagnostician." *Professional Psychology* 3, 1972, 34-40.

Lippitt, G. L. *Organizational Renewal: A Holistic Approach to Organizational Development.* 2d ed. Englewood Cliffs, N.J.: Prentice-Hall, 1982.

Lippitt, G. and Lippitt, R. *The Consulting Process in Action.* La Jolla, Cal.: University Associates, 1978.

Lippitt, G. L. and Nadler, L. "Emerging Roles of the Training Director. *Training and Development Journal*, 1967.

Margulies, N. and Raia, A. *Organizational Development: Values, Process, and Technology.* New York: McGraw-Hill, 1972.

Marguiles, N. and Raia, A. *Conceptual Foundations of Organizational Development.* New York: McGraw-Hill, 1978.

McGregor, D. *The Human Side of Enterprise.* New York: McGraw-Hill, 1960.

Menzel, R. A. "A Taxonomy of Change Agent Skills." *Journal of European Training* 4, no. 5, 1975, 287-88.

Miles, R. E. *Theories of Management: Implications for Organizational Behavior and Development.* New York: McGraw-Hill, 1975.

Mitchell, M. D. "Consultant Burnout." In J. E. Jones and J. W. Pfeiffer (eds.), *The 1974 Annual Handbook for Group Facilitations.* La Jolla, Cal.: University Associates, 1977.

Naismith, D. Unpublished Response to G. Lippitt. George Washington University, Fall, 1971. In G. Lippitt's *Organizational Renewal.* 2d ed. Englewood Cliffs, N.J.: Prentice-Hall, 1982.

Rogers, E. M. and Shoemaker, F. F. *Communication of Innovations.* 2d ed. New York: The Free Press, 1971.

Schein, E. H. *Career Dynamics: Matching Individual and Organizational Needs.* Reading, Mass.: Addison-Wesley, 1978.

Strauss, G. "Organizational Development: Credits and Debits." *Organizational Dynamics* 1, no. 3, 1973, 2-19.

Tannenbaum, R. and Davis, S. A. "Values, Man, and Organizations." *Industrial Management Review* 10, 1969, 67-86.

Tichy, N. M. "Agents of Planned Social Change: Congruence of Values, Cognitions, and Actions." *Administrative Science Quarterly* 19, no. 2, 1974, 164-82.

Varney, G. H. Developing OD Competencies. *Training and Development Journal* 34, no. 4, 1980, 30-35.

Warrick, D. D. and Donovan, T. "Surveying OD Skills." *Training and Development Journal* 33, no. 9, 1979, 22-25.

Warrick, D. D. and Thompson, J. T. "Still Crazy After All These Years." *Training and Development Journal* 34, no. 4, 1980, 16-23.

Wooten, K. C. and White, L. P. "CBID: Cognitive, Behavioral, and Interpersonal Development—A Social Learning Approach to Skill Development." *Journal of Experiential Learning and Simulation* 2, 1980, 89-99.

Zaltman, G. and Duncan, R. *Strategies for Planned Change.* New York: Wiley-Interscience, 1977.

3

Professional Ethics:
A Science, A Philosophy,
Or A Practice?

INTRODUCTION

Examination of professional ethics as it relates to the practice of organizational development is paramount to the evolution of organizational development as a legitimate profession. Many of the values upon which organizational development is based are replete with ethical questions, and organizational development practitioners are constantly encountering ethical dilemmas. Basic questions arise such as: What is professional ethics, and what relationship does it have to the organizational development profession? How should organizational development practitioners and theorists conceptualize and operationalize professional ethics? Finally, how has professional ethics evolved in other professions, and how does this relate to the current status of organizational development?

Organizational development is in a dynamic period in terms of the development of professional ethics. One obstacle that has impeded development is the heterogeneity of consultant backgrounds and technology. This manifests itself as a form of benign neglect. Benign neglect can be analyzed at the microlevel via examination of the driving and restraining forces which are currently affecting the development of professional ethics.

THE DISCIPLINE OF PROFESSIONAL ETHICS

The Study of Professional Ethics

The study of professional ethics should focus on three questions. First, professional ethics needs to be identified and classified. Is it a science, a philosophy, or a practice? Second, what is the derivation of professional ethics? More specifically, what has influenced professional ethics, and of what is professional ethics composed? Finally, how do professional ethics evolve?

The divergence in ethics ideology leaves the concept of professional ethics in a disadvantageous position. No singular approach to ethics fully illustrates the field's ideological tenets. Few scholars have tried to define professional ethics with any degree of specificity, or to describe its nature beyond simple generalities. Further, professional ethics is not a new concept, but it appears to be the area of ethics about which the least is written.

Writers such as Durkheim (1958) have tried to differentiate professional ethics from other branches of ethics. This problem is compounded because professional ethics incorporates many ideological tenets proposed by traditional ethicists. Durkheim felt that professional ethics dealt with the professional groups that developed them, and therefore they could be differentiated from other forms of ethics that dealt with society in general. "It is exactly because they govern functions not performed by everyone," writes Durkheim, "that not everyone is able to have a sense of what these functions are, of what they ought to be, or of what special relations should exist between the individuals applying them" (p. 6). All professional ethical systems are influenced by prevailing value systems of the professional group and society in general.

While one can, as Durkheim suggests, differentiate professional ethics from other forms of ethics, this differentiation should be approached with caution. That is, professional ethics is a specialized form of ethics in and of itself, and this specialization is predicted upon its inclusion of the many other forms of ethical thought. Since professional ethics incorporates many aspects of ethical thought, the study of professional ethics must attend to the impact of its historical development.

PROFESSIONAL ETHICS AS A
SPECIALIZED FORM OF ETHICS

The problem of professional ethics was first described in the early part of this century. King's (1922) foreword to the American Academy of Political and Social Sciences, followed by works of Heermance (1924) and Taeusch (1926) illustrate concern for a growing problem. These scholars were concerned about many of the growing professions and their practices upon a naive public. Their pragmatic approach to professional behavior in an industrializing society is noteworthy.

With the emergence of scientific management, social stratification as a function of occupation and training, and the importance of ideological factors within specific occupations, several observers were provoked by the obvious possibilities. King (1922) stated that

> The complexities and the specializations of modern industrial life leave many individuals unable to judge whether or not a member of any profession has performed his services with due regard to the interest of his client. In all but the most crass and obvious default in service standards, the work of the physician must be judged by physicians and that of the lawyers, by lawyers, and so with each of the professions. The higher the skill, the greater the need for organized group effort toward maintaining a fine sense of obligations, not primarily to others in the same profession, but chiefly to the general well being of all. (p. vii)

Within several years, Taeusch (1926) and Heermance (1924) were articulating similar thoughts. Heermance noted:

> Each profession or trade has its own problems of ethics. The conduct of their members must be judged by its consequences to the group itself and to the community. In the course of time there is likely to develop a certain standard of practice. Traditional customs are questioned and revised, in the light of wider experience. The association comes to have an unwritten code of honor. But there is always a fringe of unscrupulous men who are ready to disregard the accepted standard, for the sake of immediate gain. Unethical practices are not only a menace to society, they jeopardize the standing of the group as a whole, and tend to depreciate the value of its service. The enforcement of the standard becomes a matter of self preservation. (p. 1)

Much later, observers of professional ethics such as Tsanoff (1955), Durkheim (1958), and Bennion (1969) noted how emerging professions were developing in a more technological society. Concerning the immediacy with which professional ethics needed attention, Durkheim (1958) noted:

> There should be rules telling each of the workers his rights and his duties, not vaguely in general terms but in precise detail, having in view the most ordinary day to day occurrences. All these various inter-relations cannot remain forever in a state of fluctuating balance. A system of ethics, however, is not to be improvised. . . . Therefore, the true cure for the evil is to give the professional groups in the economic order a stability they so far do not possess. Whilst the craft union or corporate body is nowadays only a collection of individuals who have no lasting ties one with another, it must become and return to being a well defined and organized association. (p. 13)

Noting the differences faced in a highly technological society with new sciences and subsequent professions emerging, Tsanoff (1955) addressed its prominence in our social development. He warned that "the spreading tendencies in many occupations toward self-promotion of artisan crafts, frequently by the device of some new title, should not be music used as expression of small type vanity" (p. 281). Later, Bennion (1969) investigating the emergence of consultant professions noted that, "Problemms of health, rights, or property call for a personal relationship with a trusted advisor, whose discretion is absolute, who serves no master but his client, and whose competence is assured" (p. 16).

More recently, professional ethics have been examined by sociologists dealing with the phenomenon of professionalization among occupations (Caplow 1954, Durkheim 1958, Vollmier and Mills 1968, Bennion 1969, Harries-Jenkens 1970, Jackson 1970, Moore 1970, Pavalko 1971 and 1972, Elliot 1972, Freidson 1975, and Larson 1977). These works investigate the sequence of events that occurs in specific occupations as they become specialized and professionalized, as well as those properties which differentiate a refined profession from an occupation.

Table 3.1 illustrates several sociological models for the professionalization of various occupations. Works by Caplow (1954) and Wilensky (1964) illustrate the temporal sequence of events that occur as occupations evolve into a profession. Works by Greenwood

TABLE 3.1. Sociological Models for the Professionalization of Various Occupations

Caplow 1964	Greenwood 1972	Bennion 1969	Wilensky 1964	Harries-Jenkins 1970
1) Establishment of a professional association	1) Systematic Theory	1) An Intellectual Basis	1) People engaging in a full time activity	1) A structural element
2) Name Formulation for identity and public image	2) Authority	2) A Private Practice	2) A training school is established	2) A contextual element
3) Development of a code of ethics	3) Community sanctions	3) An Advisory Function	3) A professional association is formed	3) An activity element
4) Enactment of legal restrictions of practice	4) Ethical Codes	4) A Tradition of Service	4) Association engaged in political activity to enact laws to protect group	4) An educational element
	5) Establishment of a community	5) A Representative Institution	5) A code of ethics is developed	5) An ideological element
		6) A Code of Conduct		6) A behavioral element (code of conduct, evaluation of merit)

(1972), Harries-Jenkins (1970), and Bennion (1969) differentiate occupations from professions. These authors have specified what they consider to be the necessary elements or attributes for an occupation to be legitimately considered a profession. Of specific interest is the fact that each depicts the importance of a code of conduct or ethical code. Thus, one could argue that professionalization of various occupations is largely contingent upon having codes of conduct and formalized ethical systems, which are communicated to members of the profession and consumers of its services.

Because professional ethics has been approached from so many varied perspectives, and given that the definition and finite sequence of professionalization is debated (Harries-Jenkins, 1970; Pavalko, 1971; Barber, 1963), the concept of professional ethics is left unresolved. In fact, professional ethics itself cannot, at least from the sociological perspective, be distinctly separated from the concepts of conduct and ethical codes. Consider the following.

Greenwood (1972), attempting to differentiate between the self-regulative codes characteristic of all occupations and professional codes which are explicit, systematic, and written, concluded that

> A professional code is perhaps more explicit, systematic, and binding; it certainly possesses more altruistic overtones and is more public service oriented. These account for the frequent synonymous use of the terms professional and ethical when applied to occupational behavior. (p. 10)

Harries-Jenkins (1970), in discussing the behavior of occupational groups as they react to external and internal stimuli, maintained that

> The extent to which the group demands a common standard of behavior be adopted in relation to the task, is thus, in itself, an embryonic index of varying levels of professionalization. . . . In the most highly developed form, such contents are verbalized in the particular codes of conduct adopted by the group, and different codes of various professionalized occupational groups represent the deliberate application of generally accepted standard to particular spheres of conduct. (p. 83)

Professional ethics is clearly a specialized form of ethics. Historically, however, there has been a lack of differentiation from other forms of ethics. Ethical systems applied to occupational behavior can be seen to have been narrowly conceived, inadequately defined, and consequently misunderstood. The discipline in its current state is suffering from lack of an acceptable definition and lack of clarity with regard to its parameters.

A WORKING CONTEXT FOR PROFESSIONAL ETHICS

The Domain and Definition of Professional Ethics

The foregoing review of past and current work by traditional professional ethicists and more recent scholars has not adequately defined or specified the domains of professional ethics. The theoretical and practical differences that are conceived in varied approaches to ethics suggest five distinct, yet not mutually exclusive constructs. These five constructs are values, norms, science, laws, and ethics. Figure 3.1 illustrates the role these constructs play in specifying the domain of professional ethics.

FIGURE 3.1. The Domain of Professional Ethics

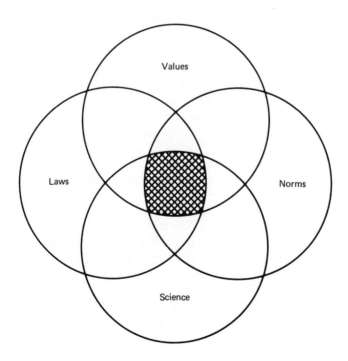

The model in Figure 3.1 proposes that professional ethics can be conceptually defined as the interaction of the values, norms, science, and laws existing within a given discipline. It follows that the development of values, norms, science, and laws are necessary prerequisites for an ethical system to exist within a profession. The problem with these constructs is that there is little academic consensus of agreement as to their absolute nature and finite definition. Each of these constructs has, however, significantly influenced the development of professional ethics in various fields. The starting point, therefore, must be an attempt to shed light on their differentiation and interrelatedness. Table 3.2 illustrates general definitions for each of these constructs. On close inspection, one can readily see the interactional components among them.

Since previous work has rarely dealt with the components of professional ethics, operational definitions have not been proposed. Professional ethics can be conceptually defined as the interaction of

TABLE 3.2. Differentiation of Various Terms Used in Describing Properties Involved in Professional Ethics

Values	Beliefs or ideals held by individuals or groups concerning what is good, right, desirable, or important in an idea, object, or action.
Norms	An idea, conceptualization, belief, or a statement enforced by the sanctions of members of a group concerning their behavioral rules, patterns, and conduct, which is referenced in the form of what should be done, what ought to be done, what is expected, and the level of action or expectation under specific circumstances.
Science	A body of knowledge that is characterized by the use of the scientific method which seeks out goal oriented information through systematic, unified, and self correcting processes.
Laws	A system of social rules, norms, or standards of behavior, concerning the right and wrong of human conduct that is put in codes enforced by sanctions imposed through recognized authority.
Ethics	Concepts and standards held by individuals or groups concerning the values surrounding the rightness and wrongness of modes of conduct in human behavior and the result of human behavior or actions.

the values, norms, science, and laws existing within a given discipline. This interaction is difficult to express on an operational basis because the values, norms, science, and laws existing within disciplines and professions differ widely.

How Professional Ethics Evolve

Scholars have given as little attention to the evolution of professional ethics as they have given to content and definition. Figure 3.2 illustrates such an attempt. Here the evolution of professional ethics must begin with values, beliefs, or ideals held by the individuals or groups in a specific discipline. As these values are developed, professional norms evolve in the form of ideas, conceptualizations, and beliefs, concerning what should be done, what ought to be done, what is expected, and levels of performance. As those norms develop, the next stage of the evolution of a professional ethic involves the development of a formal science. Here, a body of knowledge is developed based on values and norms of the members of the profession who use the scientific method to investigate phenomena in that discipline.

Based on a given discipline's values, norms, and body of knowledge, social rules and standards of behavior concerning the rights and wrongs of professional conduct emerge. Accompanying this, the enforcement of sanctions involving a recognized authority occurs.

FIG. 3.2. The Stages in the Evolution of Professional Ethics

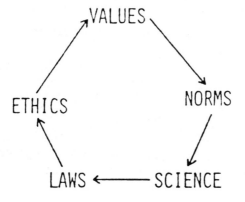

This stage is represented in Figure 3.2 as the stage of Law. Only after these values, norms, science, and laws develop, can there be said to exist professional ethics for a given discipline. As shown in Figure 3.2, each of these five stages in the development of professional ethics influences its evolution and essence.

A representative example of this evolution can be found in the evolution of professional ethics in the medical profession. Here, the values of what is good, right, important, and desirable concerning the physical well being of individuals have existed presumably as long as man has been a conscious species. Over the course of centuries, differences in these values were minimized as more advanced social groupings were formed. As civilization progressed, norms concerning the practice of healing others were developed. Witchcraft, sorcery, and healers using a variety of techniques developed specific methods for curing the ills of man.

Eventually, as advancing civilization bore the hard sciences, these scientific developments were applied to the healing of the ill. This application grew into a science that, through the scientific method, sought out the most effective means to ease pain and eliminate disease. As the science grew, and as recognized bodies, in the form of universities and medical schools became more specialized and professional, laws were enacted to enhance and protect the emerging medical profession and its clients. Recognized authority in the form of governmental legislation and professional sanctions began to emerge. Nearly all states have laws specifying who can claim to be a physician, and how they may advertise, etc. Further, the American Medical Association, as a governing body, has stringent professional laws governing the liscensing process, professional standards, and the content of professional and speciality education.

The results of these values, norms, science, and laws which have developed in the medical profession are now seen as an explicit and strict written code of ethics as developed by the American Medical Association. The AMA's code of ethics deals directly with the quality of service standards and the sanctions involved with the violation of these standards. In this way, the medical profession has the ability to specify and control the behavior of individuals practicing medicine. These ethical codes and activities of the AMA governing body specify the values, norms, science, and laws, and their appropriateness in the form of the eventual conduct and practice of its members.

As shown in Figure 3.2, each of these five stages in the developmement of professional ethics influences its evolution and development, as illustrated by the medical profession. Certainly one can cite many illustrations where human values have influenced the norms of practice in medical services. These human values and norms have dictated the course of medical science. The development of its science provided the context and basis for enacting legislation and developing laws based on the most current knowledge of medical issues. Subsequently, the values, norms, science, and laws have influenced the development of the AMA code of ethics. Moreover, the ethics now existing in the medical profession can be seen to influence the values held by its members, the norms they enforce, the science they investigate and expand, and the laws that are enacted and enforced.

The medical profession is only one of many professions that have developed a code of professional ethics. The legal profession, contemporary psychology, the engineering profession, as well as the accounting profession have all followed a similar pattern. Each has a code of ethics specifying professional standards and the sanctions involved in their violation. Each have legislative bodies who enact legislation in addition to a professional governing body determining standards that are based on the values of its membership, their norms of practice, and the expanding framework of the science of that profession. Thus, this evolutionary process can be seen to have occurred in many professions, with many other professions and emerging professions at one of the five evolutionary stages.

OD's Present Evolutionary Status

Through analysis of organizational development in terms of its evolution and professional ethics, practitioners, theorists, and professional groups can guide the profession to its eventual status as a legitimate profession. The history and current status of organizational development must be assessed before new directions are clarified.

Figure 3.2 illustrates an analytic approach to the professionalization of various disciplines. The corresponding stage of evolution is shown in each decision step in Figure 3.3. In relation to organizational development, each decision step is not absolute in terms of its completeness. For example, one can assume from the available literature (Friedlander, 1976; Connor, 1977; Tichy, 1974; Farkash, 1979) that organizational development has a relatively common value sys-

FIG. 3.3. Decision Model for Professional Ethics of Various Disciplines

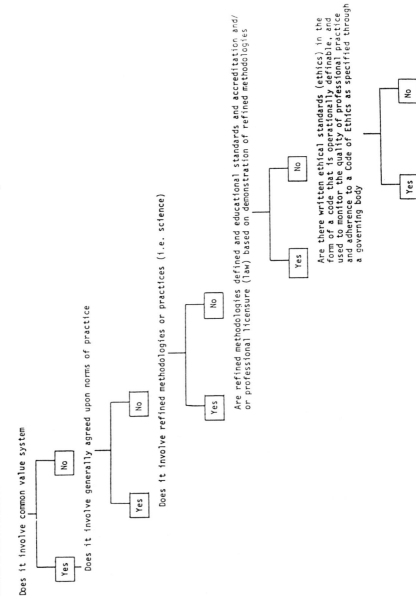

Does it involve common value system

Does it involve generally agreed upon norms of practice

Does it involve refined methodologies or practices (i.e. science)

Are refined methodologies defined and educational standards and accreditation and/or professional licensure (law) based on demonstration of refined methodologies

Are there written ethical standards (ethics) in the form of a code that is operationally definable, and used to monitor the quality of professional practice and adherence to a Code of Ethics as specified through a governing body tem. Yet, some value dilemmas are still seen to exist (Bowen, 1977). There is, however, general consensus about what is good, what is right, and what is desirable. Examples of this are trust, honesty, openness, and growth to the fullest potential of the individual and the organization. Thus, one can say that organizational development does have a common value system; however, it needs much refinement and elaboration.

The next step in the decision model involves agreed-upon norms of practice. The organizational development profession has ideas and beliefs as to what should be done, what ought to be done, what is expected, and the level of actions and expectations. This is exemplified by current literature describing the technical aspects of organizational interventions (French and Bell, 1978; Margulies and Raia, 1978; Huse, 1980), as well as comprehensive reviews of literature (White and Mitchell, 1976; Friedlander and Brown, 1974; Alderfer, 1976, 1977). To this extent, norms of practice exist in the context of the operational components of the organizational development process. That is, almost all organizational development practitioners' activities will involve some form of system diagnosis through active research and assessment, followed by actions in the form of an intervention or series of interventions, and completed with some form of what French and Bell (1978) call an ongoing process maintenance. Thus, like the area of values, norms do exist in organizational development. However, much work and refinement is needed in the area of sanctions and the level of actions and performance of those making interventions into organizations.

It is this next step of the decision model that tends to illustrate fully OD's current stage of development as a discipline. This stage of evolution begins with the building of sound organizational development theory. Weisbord (1974) illustrates the gap between Organizational Development practice, theory, and publication. He states, "If pure action is quick and dirty, and pure research is slow and clean, then action research in organizations, let alone between them, is in many ways the slowest and messiest of all, requiring as it does meticulous attention to thousands of moving parts and some simple conceptual scheme to make sense of them" (p. 477).

Elaborating further on the status of organizational development's theory base, Friedlander and Brown (1974) state:

> We have generally failed to produce a theory of change which emerges from the change process itself. We need a way of enriching our action

synergistically rather than at one or the other's expense—to become a science in which knowledge-getting and knowledge-giving are an integrated process and one that is valuable to all parties involved. We believe that a theory of planned change must be a theory of practice, which emerges from practice data and is of the practice situation, not merely about it. (p. 366)

Only in the last several years have concerted attempts been made to empirically investigate specific methodologies and practices (Porras, 1978; Bowers, 1976). The scientific method is difficult to employ in the context of the complexities in any organizational system. Identification, illustration, and replication of the nature of true cause and effect presents the greatest challenge. Further, research designs that are frequently used in the evaluation of intervention activities are often suspect when controlling sources of error. Threats to internal and external validity in experimental designs are a serious problem in the building of empirical bridges to organizational development.

Illustrating the problem of building sound intervention theory is White and Mitchell's (1976) finding that only twelve of forty-four organizational development research studies they reviewed employed experimental or quasi-experimental designs. Further, there is the problem of longitudinal research. Because organizational development is a relatively new discipline, this obviously will be a problem for some time to come. However, a review by Pate, Nielson, and Baron (1976) has shown an increase of longitudinal research in the field.

Obviously, then, the fourth and fifth step in the decision model depicted in Figure 3.3 is not complete. Without refined methodologies and practices (science), educational standards, accreditation, and professional licensure, a code of ethics cannot fully be formulated. In several cases, educational standards, accreditation, and professional licensure do exist. For example, entry into several organizational development professionals associations is based on possession of advanced degrees. Degree content, however, is not specified. Organizations such as the American Society of Personnel Administrators have accrediting examinations for those in the area of training and development. Further, most professional organizations that have some form of licensure process for those practicing organizational development have a written code of ethics. However, none have developed their codes of ethics operationally to facilitate monitoring of actions. As one might expect, then, the sanctions used to monitor the quality of practitioners' actions do not exist.

PROFESSIONAL ETHICS IN OD

Benign Neglect

Although there has recently been increased activity to explore the issue of professional ethics in OD, there have been many obstacles that have impeded the development of professional ethics. Contemporary texts by Lippitt and Lippitt (1978), French and Bell (1978), and Lippitt (1982) have devoted attention to the subject. Articles and manuscripts by Walton and Warwick (1973), Benne (1959), Maidment and Losito (1980), Pfeiffer and Jones (1977), Warwick and Kelman (1973), Zaltman and Duncan (1976), Wooten and White (1983), and White and Wooten (1983) have considered various ethical dilemmas encountered by the change agent and the client system. This increased popularity can be seen as a direct result of the identity crises that OD has experienced as it has attempted to define its priorities.

Benne (1959) has taken the position that a consultant should face, recognize, articulate, and rationally solve his own ethical questions. This approach to resolving ethical questions is inextricably linked to the heterogeneity of consultant backgrounds, thereby making any sort of homogeneity of solution virtually unworkable and apparently impossible. Warwick and Kelman (1973) have noted these difficulties and have argued for a more consistent set of standards, although they do not go to the extreme of supporting a moratorium on practice, Walton and Warwick (1973) maintain that a more profitable root to ethical understanding is more deliberation: that is, continued practice coupled with self-analysis and dialogue.

Other scholars (Mosely, 1970; Zaltman and Duncan, 1977; Warwick and Kelman, 1973; Pfeiffer and Jones, 1977; and Maidment and Losito, 1980) have all expressed concerns about the value and ethical dilemmas faced by the consultant as the utilization of the consultative process continues to increase. White and Wooten (1983) assert that ethical systems for OD, as well as other professions, undergo an evolutionary process, that this process can be utilized as it occurs, and that rational conclusions can be drawn from systematic observation and concomitant analysis. Further, this observation and analysis includes the client system as a mutual partner in this ethicality of OD actions and interest.

From the available literature, at least one major conclusion can be drawn pertaining to ethical dilemmas that face the interventionist. This variable is the heterogeneity of consultant background, values, and discipline. This heterogeneity has caused consultants to rely upon their fields of origin in resolving ethical dilemmas, creating either a nonapplicability or a nonacceptance attitude. A corollary to this conclusion is the idea that heterogeneity of background and discipline has created a situation where there is little consensus of thought, philosophy, and technology. The greatest emphasis has been on the technology of OD and correctly so when one looks at the development of professional ethics as an evolutionary process.

Increased attention to professional ethics has been and will continue to be paid by professional organizations whose membership constitutes the OD profession. Organizations such as the American Psychological Association, the OD Network, the Academy of Management—OD Division, Certified Consultant International and the International Registry of Organizational Development Professionals all have written codes, or are presently in the process of developing them. The major difficulty is that memberships in any of these professional organizations is not required in order to practice OD. However, monitoring and adherence to such codes is typically left to the individual practitioner.

A result of the heterogeneity of consultant background, education, professional affiliation, and technology appears to be a form of benign neglect of professional ethics. Hypothetically, this relationship could be stated as follows: "When differential rates of knowledge develop in a given discipline, then the professional ethics surrounding that discipline will not develop until the values and norms are specific, the science is developed, and laws governing practice and use of the discipline are adhered to." An important indicator of professionalization of a science is increased discussion about the development of an ethical system. This is the point at which the OD profession finds itself presently.

Forces Affecting the Development of Professional Ethics

OD is in a dynamic period in terms of the development of professional ethics. A variety of forces are both negatively and positively affecting development. As shown in Figure 3.4, the current status of professional ethics in OD can be illustrated by a force-field analysis. This force-field analysis depicts both driving and restraining forces which are assisting and impeding the development of professional ethics. The driving forces and restraining forces have been operating since the emergence of OD itself. However, within the last decade, these forces have had significantly greater impact on the OD profession.

As shown in Figure 3.4, there are five driving forces. These are activities which increase the effort to refine and expose professional ethics in OD. The first driving force is maturation of OD as a science. This action is best illustrated by the high numbers of empirical and longitudinal research studies now being produced (Porras and Berg, 1978), although the level of research rigor is somewhat questionable (White and Mitchell, 1976). More often than not, the use of sound experimental design and multivariate statistical techniques are being utilized. Further, replications of interventions and comparative analysis are increasing in frequency.

The second driving force which enhances efforts to develop ethics in OD is the practice of ad hoc ethical norms. Here, inappropriate decisions and situational ethics on the part of both change agent and client systems have caused increased concern. Interventions with inconsistent approaches to issues involving confidentiality of information, manipulation of organizational participants, and the lack of proper skills and knowledge have increased attention and pressure.

The third driving force is the increase in professionalization among OD practitioners themselves. The growth in membership in professional associations has been steady over the past two decades. Simultaneously, the number of workshops for OD practitioners has grown. Further, the number of professional publications for OD practioners has grown tremendously. This has culminated in OD practioners regarding themselves as professionals in the same way physicians and lawyers do.

The fourth driving force causing increased pressure on the OD field to develop its ethics is the increased need for OD services. The

FIG. 3.4. Force Field Analysis of the Current Status of Professional Ethics in Organizational Development

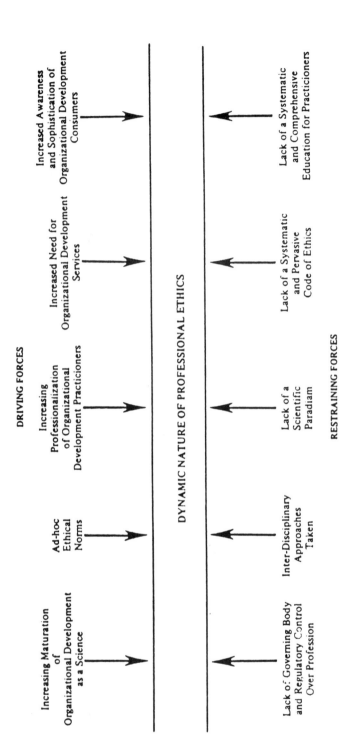

Source: From Wooten, K. C. and White, L. P. "Ethical Problems in the Practice of Organization Development." *Training and Development Journal* 37, no. 4, 1983, p. 17.

growth and demand for OD programs and consultants has increased yearly, as organizational life has become more turbulent. Bennis (1969) found three reasons for this increasing need. They are: (1) the need for new organizational forms; (2) the focus of cultural change; and (3) the increase in social awareness. These needs are coupled with an everchanging workforce, the complexity of organizational structure, and rapid technological and produce obsolescence.

The fifth driving force is the increasing sophistication of the client base. Increasing numbers of client systems have had experience with OD interventions, and subsequently have altered expectations. Simultaneously, the management and workforce of most organizations is much more educated than ever before, with many line managers now possessing an M.B.A. degree. Therefore, client systems expect a high degree of sophistication from professionals working in the OD field.

Figure 3.4 also shows restraining forces, or those forces which negatively affect efforts to develop professional ethics in the OD field. The first restraining force is the lack of a universally accepted governing body or regulatory control over the OD profession. While some states have legislation that regulates entry into the consultation field, by and large, anyone may enter the OD profession. Additionally, professional associations who have practitioners as members do not and cannot control their professional behavior. The second restraining force is the interdisciplinary population which constitutes the OD profession. As previously stated, the heterogeneity of background, education, values, and technologies produces inconsistencies in the approaches taken by OD practitioners. Subsequently, many people have entered the OD field, bringing with them their values, orientation, and approaches developed from their previous experiences and professional activities. At the same time, this heterogeneity of background is a rich and varied source of influence which reduces "tunnel vision" on the part of the OD community in general.

The third restraining force inhibiting ethical development for OD is the lack of a true scientific paradigm for OD researchers and practitioners. Because generalized methodologies and evaluation models cannot be universally applied to any organization, definitive standards of practice have not fully developed. Although the use of group experiential and experimental designs have increased, the volume of variables in any organization acts as a source of error, thereby producing inconclusive results. Based on Kuhn's (1970) notion of science, OD is at the outside of what is, and perhaps what should be, considered a normal science.

The fourth restraining force inhibiting fuller development of ethics for the OD profession is the lack of a specific code of ethics which is acceptable to the majority of OD practitioners. While existing codes among professional organizations are becoming increasingly refined, none have an adequate form of monitoring should their code be broken. Additionally, many of the codes are elusive, that is, not specific enough to determine appropriateness of behavior. Most existing codes are statements of values or guides for professional behavior.

The fifth restraining force consists of a lack of systematic and comprehensive education for practitioners. While there are increasing numbers of OD-related degree programs, continuing education programs, and accrediting institutions, the vast number of practitioners have been self-educated in OD theory and practice. This condition is compounded by the fact that there is little agreement as to what educational criteria OD programs should utilize. Thus, there is, and will continue to be, tremendous divergence in practice and theory.

SUMMARY

Professional ethics can be seen as a separate discipline, yet it is closely related to other norms of ethical study. The dependence and interrelatedness of values, norms, science, and laws form the essence of professional ethics. Each of these constructs plays an indispensable role in the formulation and maintenance of professional ethical systems. Various occupations can be seen to have evolved through various stages in which professional ethics exist to varying degrees.

Professional ethics can therefore be defined as the identification of the values, norms, science, and laws within a given discipline. The logical extension of this argument is that the development of values, norms, science, and laws are necessary prerequisites to the development of an ethical system. Through analysis of the development process of organizational development, a determination can be made concerning where organizational development is in its development. The benign neglect proposition was explored as an explanation for the lack of an ethical system in the OD profession. A force-field analysis was performed to better analyze specific forces and how they operate upon the development of OD.

NOTES

Alderfer, C. P. "Organizational Development." *Annual Review of Psychology* 28, 1977, 197–283.

Alderfer, C. P. "Change Processes in Organizations." In M.D. Dunnette (ed.), *Handbook of Industrial Organizational Psychology.* Chicago: Rand McNally, 1976.

Barber, B. "Is American Business Becoming Professionalized? Analysis of A Social Ideology." In Edward A. Tiryakian (ed.), *Sociological Theory, Values, and Socio-Cultural Change.* New York: Free Press, 1963, 121–45.

Benne, K. D. "Some Ethical Problems in Group and Organizational Consultation." *Journal of Social Issues* 15, no. 2, 1959, 60-67.

Bennion, F. A. *Professional Ethics: The Consultant Professions and Their Code.* London: Charles Knight and Co., 1969.

Bennis, W. G. *Organization Development: Its Nature, Origins and Prospects.* Reading, Mass.: Addison-Wesley, 1969.

Bowen, D. D. "Value Dilemmas in Organizational Development." *Journal of Applied Behavior Science* 13, no. 13, 1977, 543-56.

Bowers, D. G. "Organizational Development: Promises, Performance, Possibilities." *Organizational Dynamics* 4, 1976, 50-62.

Caplow, T. *The Sociology of Work.* Minneapolis: University of Minnesota Press, 1954.

Connor, P. E. "A Critical Inquiry into Some Assumptions and Values Characterizing O.D." *The Academy of Management Review* 2, no. 4, 1977, 635-44.

Durkheim, E. *Professional Ethics and Civil Morals.* New York: Free Press of Glencoe, 1958.

Elliot, P. *The Sociology of Professions.* New York: Hunder and Hunder, 1972.

Farkash, A. *An Empirical Investigation of Organizational Development Beliefs, Activities, and Outcomes.* Selected Paper No. 8. Madison, Wis.: American Society for Training and Development, 1979.

Freidson, E. (ed.) *The Professions and Their Prospects*, Beverly Hills, CA.: Sage Publications, 1975.

French, W. L. and Bell, C. H., Jr. *Organizational Development*. Englewood Cliffs, N.J.: Prentice-Hall, 1978.

Friedlander, F. *Purpose and Values in O.D.: Toward Personal Theory and Practice*. Madison, Wis.: American Society for Training and Development, 1976.

Friedlander, F. and Brown, L. D. "Organizational Development." *Annual Review of Psychology* 25, 1974, 313-41.

Greenwood, E. "Attributes of a Profession," in R. M. Pavalko (ed.), *Sociological Perspectives on Occupations*. Itaska, Ill.: F. E. Peacock Publishers, 1972, 3-16.

Harries-Jenkins, G. Professionals in Organizations in J. A. Jackson (ed.), *Professions and Professionalism*. London: Cambridge University Press, 1970, 53-107.

Heermance, E. L. *Code of Ethics*. Burlington, Vt.: Free Press Printing, 1924.

Huse, E. F. *Organization Development and Change*. St. Paul: West, 1980.

Jackson, J. A. *Professions and Their Professionalization*. London: Cambridge University Press, 1970.

King, C. L. "Foreword to the Ethics of the Professions and of Business." *The Annals of the American Academy of Political and Social Science*, 1922, 101, 190, vii.

Kuhn, T. S. *The Structure of Scientific Revolutions*. Chicago: The University of Chicago Press, 1970.

Larson, M. D. *The Rise of Professionalism: A Sociological Analysis*. Berkeley, Ca.: University of California Press, 1977.

Lippitt, G. L. *Organization Renewal: A Holistic Approach to Organization Development*. 2d ed. Englewood Cliffs, N.J.: Prentice-Hall, 1982.

Lippitt, R. K. and Lippitt, G. L. *The Consulting Process in Action*. La Jolla, Cal.: University Associates, 1978.

Maidment, R. and Losito, W. *Ethics and the Consultant/Trainer.* Selected Paper no. 11. Madison, Wis.: American Society for Training and Development, 1980.

Marulies, M. and Raia, A. *Conceptual Foundations of Organizational Development.* New York: McGraw-Hill, 1978.

Moore, W. E. *The Professions: Roles and Rules.* New York: Russel Sage Foundation, 1970.

Mosely, D. C. "Professional Ethics and Competencies in Management Consulting." *California Management Review* 12, no. 7, 1970, 44–48.

Pate, L. E., Nielsen, W. R., and Baron, P. C. "Advances in Research and Organizational Development: Toward a Beginning." In R. L. Taylor, M. J. O'Connell, R. A. Zawacki, and D. D. Warwick (eds.), *Academy of Management Proceedings '76* (Proceedings of the 36th Annual Meeting of the Academy of Management, Kansas City, Mo., August 11-14, 1976) 389-94.

Pavalko, R. M. *Sociology of Occupations and Professions.* Itasca, Ill.: F. E. Peacock Publishers, 1971.

Pavalko, R. M. (ed.). *Sociological Perspectives on Occupations.* Itasca, Ill.: F. E. Peacock Publishers, 1972.

Pfeiffer, J. W. and Jones, J. E. "Ethical Considerations in Consulting." In J. E. Jones and J. W. Pfeiffer (eds.), *The 1977 Handbook for Group Facilitators.* La Jolla, CA.: University Associates, 1977.

Porras, J. I. "The Impact of Organization Development. Research Findings." *Academy of Management Review* 3, no. 2, 1978, 249-66.

Porras, J. I. and Berg, P. D. "Evaluation Methodology in Organizational Development: An Analysis and Critique." *Journal of Applied Behavioral Science* 14, no. 2, 1978, 151-63.

Taeusch, C. F. *Professional and Business Ethics.* New York: Henry Holt and Co., 1926.

Tichy, N. "Agents of Planned Change: Congruence of Values, Cognitions, and Action." *Administrative Science Quarterly* 19, no. 2, 1974, 164-82.

Tsanoff, R. A. *Ethics,* New York: Harper Row, 1955.

Vollmier, H. M., and Mills, D. L. *Professionalization.* Englewood Cliffs, N.J.: Prentice-Hall, 1968.

Walton, R. E. and Warwick, D. P. "The ethics of organizational development." *Journal of Applied Behavioral Science* 9, no. 3, 1973, 681–99.

Warwick, D. P. and Kelman, H. C. "Ethics in Social Intervention." In G. Zaltman (ed.), *Processes and Phenomena of Social Change.* New York: Wiley Interscience, 1973, 377–449.

Weisbord, M. R. "The Gap Between O.D. Practice and Theory and Publication." *The Journal of Applied Behavioral Science* 10, no. 4, 1974, 476–81.

White, L. P. and Wooten, K. D. "Ethical Dilemmas in Various Stages of Organizational Development." *Academy of Management Review* 1, no. 2, 1983, 57–73.

White, S. E. and Mitchell, T. R. Organizational Development: A Review of Research Content and Research Design. *The Academy of Management Review* 2, 1976, 57–73.

Wilensky, H. L., "The Professionalization of Everyone." *The American Journal of Sociology* 70, no. 2, 1964, 137–158.

Wooten, K. D. and White, L. P. "Ethical Problems in the Practice of Organizational Development." *Training and Development Journal*, April 1983, 16–23.

Zaltman, G. and Duncan, R. "Ethics in Social Change." In G. Zaltman and R. Duncan (eds.), *Strategies for Planned Change.* New York: John Wiley and Sons, 1977, 323–77.

4

Professional Roles
and Practices

INTRODUCTION

In looking at ethical decisions and professional issues in the practice of Organizational Development, one is essentially faced with two major problems: first, to use a common and acceptable framework to describe change agent and client system behavior; second, to use an acceptable and generalizable model of the stages involved in organizational change which involves the microanalysis of the relationship between the change agent and the client system. Only when a framework to address such problems is developed, can substantive efforts be directed towards professional issues inhibiting the full utilization of OD efforts.

This chapter will explore the use of a widely used framework to analyze the behavior of organizational participants and apply it to OD. From such a focus, roles of the change agent, roles of the client system, and mutual roles will be analyzed with an emphasis placed on the impact of change roles upon the effectiveness of an intervention. Stages of the OD process will also be explored as it relates to OD practice and theory. Finally, an alternative model of change will be illustrated, depicting the prescriptive roles of change agents and client systems as they progress through a change effort.

A ROLE EPISODIC PERSPECTIVE

Use of Role Theory

One of the most widely accepted models to investigate human behavior in organizations today is role theory. Role theory as proposed by Katz and Kahn (1966) bridges both personal and social behavior by illustrating their interaction, and viewing behavior of individuals in a social or organizational context as a number of role systems, involving themselves in role episodes. This approach allows the investigator to analyze the behavior of not only the individual, but of the social system as well. The use of role theory to explain a broad range of organizational behavior is neither new (House and Rizzo, 1972; Kahn, Wolfe, Quinn, Snoek, and Rosenthal, 1964; Rizzo, House, and Lietzman, 1970), nor undocumented as evidenced by its popularity as a research tool (Szilagyi, Sims, and Keller, 1976; Bernardin, 1979; Tracy and Johnson, 1981). More recently, role theory has been used to investigate ethical dilemmas in organizational research (Mirvis and Seashore, 1979), and organizational development (Wooten and White, 1983; White and Wooten, 1983).

It appears that analyses of the behavior of change agents and client systems can best be accomplished when viewed as a role system. To do this, it is necessary to analyze the relationship of role episodes and role systems to organizational development. The role episodic model is illustrated in Figure 4.1. As shown, the role episode includes both a role sender and a role receiver, or a focal person. The role episode represents a continuous cycle of sending, receiving, responding, and the sending of new interaction. Related to organizational development, role sending and role receiving can be seen as a continuous cycle of role episodes on the part of change agents and client systems.

The designation of role sender and focal person serves as a means of identification to view a sequence of ongoing behavior, since every person in an interaction or exchange is a role sender and a role receiver for others. Because of the dynamics of interactional exchange, the person as a role sender or a focal person is interchangeable. Applied to organizational development, both the change agent and a member of the client system can assume the role of role sender or focal person. In this regard, the client system may be a group of upper managers, a functional work team, or the entire organization.

FIG. 4.1. The Role Episode

Role senders		Focal person	
Expectations	Sent role	Received role	Role behavior
Perception of focal person's behavior; evaluation	Information; attempts at influence	Perception of role, and perception of role sending	Compliance; resistance; "side effects"
I	II	III	IV

Source: From Katz, D. and Kahn, R. L. *The Social Psychology of Organizations.* New York: John Wiley and Sons, 1966, p. 182.

Figure 4.1 also depicts that the role episode comprises four concepts. These four concepts are role expectations, sent role, received role, and role behavior. These concepts are described by Katz and Kahn as follows:

> Role expectations, which are evaluative standards applied to the behavior of any person who occupies a given organizational office or position; sent role, which consist of communications stemming from role expectations and sent by members of the role set as attempts to influence the focal person; received role, which is the focal person's perception of the role-sendings addressed to him, including those he sends himself; and role behavior, which is the response of the focal person to the complexity of information he has received. (p. 182).

Using the role episode model, the behavior of change agents and client systems as role senders and focal persons, can therefore be investigated and explained. According to Katz and Kahn, role expectations and sent roles have to do with motivation, cognitions, and behaviors of the role sender. The received role and role behavior have to do with the cognitions, motivation, and behavior of the focal person. Thus, one can make reference to much of what occurs in organizational development between change agents and client systems in terms of role sending and role receiving as a continuous series of role episodes.

Since the role episodic model may greatly oversimplify the various factors which influence the behavior of the change agent and client systems, the Katz and Kahn enlargement of a role system is more fully representative. As shown in Figure 4.2, the context of role behavior should be thought of as representing all elements of the organizational system. Essentially, this model depicts the factors involved in the taking of organizational roles. Expanding the notion of a role episode, various enduring properties and characteristics that reside in the situation where the role episode occurs are shown. Three classes of properties and characteristics are represented. These three are organization, personality, and interpersonal relations.

FIG. 4.2. Expanded Model of the Role Episode

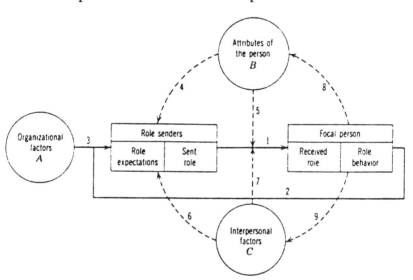

Source: From Katz, D. and Kahn, R. L. *The Social Psychology of Organizations.* New York: John Wiley and Sons, 1966, p. 182.

Figure 4.2 illustrates the influence of the organization, the person, and interpersonal relations on the role sender and the focal person. Organizational factors, personality, and interpersonal factors interact in significant ways that influence role expectations, sent role, received role, and subsequent role behavior. Related to organizational development, organizational factors, such as size, climate, technology, managerial policy, market position, and readiness to change would be definite influences upon the role episodes between the change agent and the client system. Personality factors such as learning ability, skills, perception, motives, and values likewise intervene and modify the influences of organizational factors on role behavior. Moreover, the quality and nature of interpersonal relations between the role sender and focal person will modify and influence the eventual role behavior of the change agent and client system.

Along with the singular role episode and the expanded role episode system, Katz and Kahn's notion of role conflict and role ambiguity is especially helpful in investigating the behavior of change agents. Role conflict is defined as "the simultaneous occurrence of two (or more) role sendings such that compliance with one would make more difficult compliance with the other" (Katz and Kahn, p. 184). Thus, role conflict is that conflict which arises when a person in a role episode receives incompatible messages regarding his/her desired role behavior. Katz and Kahn have identified the five types of role conflict illustrated in Table 4.1.

TABLE 4.1. Various Types of Role Conflicts

1. *Intrasender Conflict*	When expectations from a single member of a role set is incompatible, inconsistent or unrealistic.
2. *Intersender Conflict*	When expectations sent from one role sender are conflictual with the expectations of other role senders.
3. *Interrole Conflict*	When sent expectations for one role are conflicting with another role played by the same person.
4. *Person-Role Conflict*	When role requirements may violate moral or ethical values of the focal person.
5. *Role Overload*	Where the focal person is overwhelmed by requests from members of his/her role set.

Due to the number and nature of the roles assumed by change agent and client systems, as well as the nature of their interactions and exchanges, role conflict is a frequent occurrence. Not only do roles on the part of the change agent and client systems change, but also their role sets. Additionally, changing organizational factors, differing attributes of role set members, as well as their interpersonal factors contribute greatly to the occurrence of role conflict. Since the very nature of OD is based on change, and in many cases changing roles, it is quite natural that various forms of conflict will occur. Thus, both the change agent and the client system are equally as prone to experience a variety of role conflict, singularly and simultaneously.

Role Constructs and Their Application

An example of the role episode process applied to organizational development could hypothetically involve the change agent as a role sender, and a client system as the focal person or role receiver. Here, consider a change agent involved in process consultation with the board of directors of a large company. Consider the change agent's sent role as being the information, or attempts at influence, involving suggestions to the chairman of the board that he/she is dominating the decision-making process. The role receiver or the focal person (CEO) receives this and perceives it and the way it was sent, by the role sender (change agent). The CEO's role behavior would then be one of compliance, or resistance to the change agent's request to alter his/her authoritarian and centralized decision-making style. This role in turn, will be perceived and evaluated by the role sender. This action will therefore promote a new sent role by the change agent to influence the decision-making style of the CEO, thereby starting a new role episode.

Another example of how role theory may be applied to organization development could involve the client system as the role sender, and the change agent as the focal person or role receiver. Consider an organization involved in a team-building effort between various section heads of a large and loosely structured R&D department. Here, the sent role from the client system could be attempts to influence the change agent of a particular section's difficulties working on a project with other sections. The focal person (role receiver), in this case being the change agent, would then perceive this role information on its merits, and act accordingly. The change agent's compliance (agreement) or resistance to such information would then act as feedback to the client system, or role sender, which would then set up expectations for subsequent sent roles.

So too can organizational, personality, and interpersonal variables be applied in OD. In the case of the team-building effort, a host of organizational, personality, and interpersonal variables can be illustrated as to their impact on the relationship between the change agent and the client system. The organizational norm for managing departmental conflict will greatly influence the role episodes between the change agent and the client system. Attributes of the person, as a role sender or role receiver, will additionally moderate role episodes between change parties. A change agent's sensitivities, fears, and operative values impinge upon his/her attempts to influence the client. Additionally, the quality of the interpersonal relations between the role sender and the focal person will significantly moderate the status of the change agent and client system relationship. Trust, risk taking, etc., can be seen as integral factors between the parties that wield consider influence.

Role conflict can also be applied to many examples in organizational development. Change agents frequently experience intrasender conflict when the client system sends incompatiable or unrealistic role requests. An illustrative example would be requests to achieve system-wide change, yet having accessibility only to select subsystems. Another frequent example of role conflict is where the change agent experiences intersender conflict. Here, expectations sent from one subsystem (role sender) conflict with another subsystem.

Interrole conflict, person-role conflict, and role overload are also frequently experienced in OD. Interrole conflict on the part of change agents often occurs when he/she is expected to be a nurturing person, while at the same time having to confront others about negative aspects of their behavior. Change agents also frequently experience person-role conflict when role requirements request them to violate moral or ethical values. Instances where role senders or client systems request that confidentiality be broken involving survey results are a source of conflict for the change agent or focal person. Role overload is exemplified by members of a client system, who as a result of an OD intervention are overwhelmed by role requests from various organizational members and change agents.

ROLES OF THE CHANGE RELATIONSHIP

The Impact of Roles on OD Effectiveness

In any change effort, both the change agent and the client system must play a variety of singular and mutual roles. It can be argued that the extent to which these roles are played greatly determines not only the change relationship, but the effectiveness of the change effort itself. Given the highly dynamic nature of a change effort, a thorough examination of change roles is needed. According to Bell and Nadler (1976) "an understanding of the roles in the client-consultant relationship is important in order to: (1) aid both parties in the search; (2) specify mutual expectations and minimize confusion; and (3) help the consultant identify skills and competencies associated with different roles" (p. 39).

Figure 4.3 illustrates the impact of change roles upon the effectiveness of an OD intervention. It builds upon Katz and Kahn's (1966) notion that roles are greatly influenced by personality, interpersonal, and organizational factors. Figure 4.3 illustrates influences upon change roles, as well as how the change roles influence the OD process. As shown, the role of the change agent and the client system are greatly influenced by personal values, goals, needs, skills/abilities, and available resources. Additionally, the internal and external climate of an organization will greatly influence the type and nature of the roles played by change agents and client systems.

Also shown in Figure 4.3 is the influence of change roles upon an intervention's goals, strategies, and targets, as well as means and methods. These influences subsequently affect the effectiveness of the intervention itself. Although an organization's internal and external climate does wield considerable influence upon not only the change roles and the subsequent goals, strategies, targets, and methods and means, it is the relationship between the change roles and the component parts of an intervention that are noteworthy. Not only do roles of change agents and client systems influence the goals, strategies, targets, and the means and methods, but a reciprocal influence of goals or methods used which dictates appropriate change roles for effective OD.

Figure 4.3 can be used as a causal model for exploring the effects of change roles in any intervention. For example, consider how the role of a change agent is influenced by personal values for growth, skills/abilities for conducting certain types of OD, as well as personal needs and goals for performing professionally and providing the client with a usable change technology. Simultaneously, consider how an organization's internal climate such as lines of authority, risk, conflict management, tolerance for individual differences, goal orientation, performance pressures, etc. influence the roles to be played.

FIG. 4.3. The Impact of Change Roles upon the Effectiveness of Organizational Development

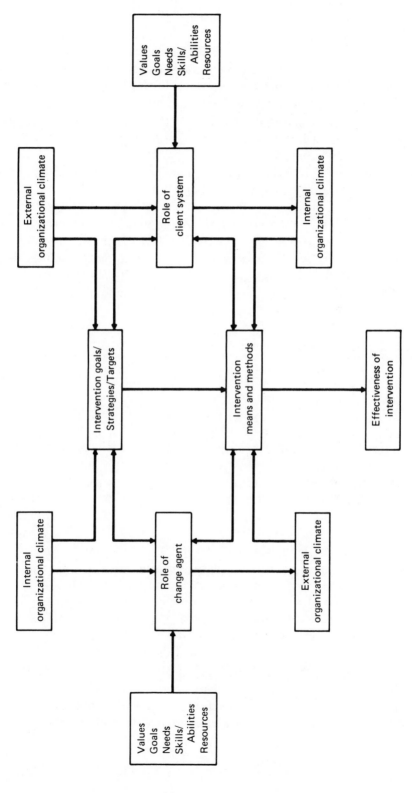

Further, factors in the external climate such as market growth, governmental regulation, competition, and resource availability, will exert considerable influence upon the change roles as well as strategies/targets and the intervention means and methods.

Figure 4.3 further illustrates that if the role of the change agent is to be only a trainer versus a process oriented consultant, this will undoubtedly alter the goals/strategies/targets, and the means and methods used. If the role of the client system is participative or passively resistant, this too will yield considerable influence. Subsequently, all the factors illustrated will influence the eventual effectiveness of the intervention itself. An argument can be made that the effectiveness of an intervention is therefore contingent upon the congruence between the personal factors (values, goals, skills/abilities, etc.), the change roles, the internal and external climate, and the intervention goals, strategies, targets, and means and methods.

Roles of the Change Agent

A variety of authors and theorists have identified the various roles of the consultant. Argyris (1970), Blake and Mouton (1976), Bennis (1973), and Lawrence and Lorsch (1969) have all reflected upon the various roles of the consultant, especially as it relates to intervention techniques and methods. In each case, emphasis is placed on the multiplicity of change roles. Lippitt and Lippitt (1976) state that "when helping other individuals, groups, organizations, or large social systems, consultants behave in a number of roles that they judge to be appropriate for the client, the situation, and the helpers own style" (p. 27).

Although there is a lack of total agreement concerning the specific roles of a consultant, there is a similarity in the terminology used to describe their behavior (Bell and Nadler, 1979). A comparative analysis of the roles played by change agents according to various theorists is illustrated in Table 4.2. As shown, Lippitt and Lippitt (1976) have identified eight specific change roles. These roles are objective observer/reflector, process counselor, fact finder, alternative identifier and linker, joint problem solver, trainer/educator, informational expert, and advocate. Havelock (1973) through exploring educational curricula for change agents has identified four major roles. These roles are catalyst, solution giver, process helper,

TABLE 4.2. Comparison of Primary Roles Played by the Change Agent

Lippitt and Lippitt (1976)	Havelock (1972)	Saskin (1974)	Menzel (1975)	Nadler (1970)	Steele (1968)
Observor/ Reflector	Catalyst	Consultant	Educator	Advocate	Teacher
Process Counselor	Solution Giver	Trainer	Diagnostician	Expert	Student
Fact Finder	Process Helper	Researcher	Consultant	Stimulator	Detective
Alternative Identifier and Linker	Resource Linker		Linker	Change Agent	Barbarian
Joint Problem Solver					Clock
Trainer/Educator					Monitor
Information Expert					Talisman
Advocate					Advocate
					Ritual Pig

and resource linker. Nadler (1970), in exploring consultant roles for human resource development practitioners, elaborates on four specific subroles. These roles are advocate, expert, stimulator, and change agent.

Steele (1975), Menzel (1975), and Saskin (1974) have also elaborated upon the roles to be played by the change agent. Steele (1975) has outlined nine roles of the consultant. These are teacher, student, detective, barbarian, clock, monitor, talisman, advocate, and ritual pig. Similarly, Menzel (1975) has identified roles consisting of educator, diagnostician, consultant, and linker. Saskin (1974) has identified these roles as consultant, trainer, and researcher. Saskin builds upon these three basic roles, depending upon the goals of the change agent. Aims or goals of the change agent according to Saskin, result in adoptive models or adaptive models. Adaptive models are those that are concerned with producing specific change, whereas adoptive are oriented toward development of the adaptive capacity of the client system to its problems.

Given the common roles illustrated by most authors, it is suggested that change agents should assume five basic change roles. These roles are educator/trainer, model, researcher/theoretician, technical expert, and resource linker.

Educator/Trainer

It is the primary task of the change agent to educate members of the client system so that the client system may adapt to needed change, whatever the scope. This role must be portrayed in a way that assists others to learn how to learn, and subsequently assume responsibility for their own learning process. This may be fulfilled through the design of learning events, services, and activities of various types. This role is related to Lippitt and Lippitt's (1976) notion of trainer/educator, Steele's (1968) notion of teacher, Menzel's (1975) notion of educator, and Saskin's (1974) notion of trainer.

Model

As the focal point in producing change, the change agent must model appropriate behaviors for organizational members to learn from. Behaviors such as risk taking, trust, and openness must be demonstrated by the change agent if such behaviors are the goal of the intervention. Here, the change agent must advocate change, yet remain sensitive to the values surrounding his/her profession.

Researcher/Theoretician

Crucial to the task of effective organizational change is that objective data and perceptions be gathered in a systematic and scientific manner. Since most organizational problems are complex and changing, a variety of research skills must be drawn upon for accurate diagnosis. Based on collections of objective diagnosis data, it is the change agent's role to make sense of it all. Here, a change agent's ability to build behavioral models and to map the future are essential. This role is closely related to Lippitt and Lippitt's (1976) notion of observer/reflector and fact finder, Steele's (1968) notion of detective, Menzel's (1975) notion of diagnostician, and Saskin's (1976) notion of researcher.

Technical Expert

The most obvious role to be assumed by a change agent is as a provider of special skills, knowledge, or expertise. Here, the role of technical expert involves the acquisition and use of information in accordance with the goals of the change effort. This expertise must span not only specialty areas of change technology, but the management of the change process as well. More specifically, the wisdom of where and when to apply information is of major importance. This role is closely related to Menzel's (1975) concept of consultant, Lippitt and Lippitt's (1976) idea of information expert, and Nadler's (1970) concept of expert.

Resource Linker

A truly healthy organization should know and properly use the resources at its disposal. Often, only the objective perspective of a change agent can identify needed resources, and link them in a meaningful and productive fashion. Resources may be material or non-material, but most often deal with information about people and their specific needs. This role relates to Lippitt and Lippitt's (1976) idea of identifier and linker, but more specifically to Havelock's (1975) notion of resource linker, and Menzel's (1975) notion of linker.

Roles of the Client System

Based on the notion that change agents have major roles to assume during an organizational intervention, so should client systems have major roles to assume. However, the roles to be assumed by a client system are somewhat different. These roles are in direct relation to roles to be assumed by the change agent, as well as in relation to who and what the client system wishes to become. Unfortunately, as noted by Bell and Nadler (1979) "there is a severe lack of material concerning the roles of the client" (p. 39).

Exploring the differences in roles to be played by change agents and client systems, Steele (1968) draws several interesting conclusions. He states "to begin with, the concept of client is an abstraction used by consultants so that they know how to refer to people that they are trying to help. Clients do not necessarily think of themselves as clients at all. They almost always have more important identities as businessmen, scientist, or government officials" (p. 40). Nevertheless, Steele suggests that the client system should portray the roles of student, good citizen, and performer.

Rather than passive observers, or resistant pockets of power, at least four proactive roles should be assumed by the client system. These roles are resource provider, supporter/advocate, information supplier, and participant. Each of these roles assumes that the OD effort is a collaborative effort on the part of the change effort and the client system to assist the organization to cope with and manage change.

Resource Provider

In order for the change intervention to reach its goals, the client system must provide the needed resources to the change agent and to those making the change. Resources involving money, time, and accessibility are all crucial to the eventual outcome of the change effort.

Supporter/Advocate

Client system support is necessary for the organizational change. Unless sufficient numbers of the organization believe change is necessary, and unless key members of management provide adequate reinforcers for behavior change, it will be either resisted or short-lived. Therefore, client systems should be advocates of change, while avoiding unnecessary change.

Information Supplier

One of the more crucial roles for members of an entire client system to assume is information supplier. Due to the risk involved in providing information involving self and others, information is the commodity upon which accurate data and perceptions are based. With accurate data and clear perceptions of the organization, the necessary reality testing can take place.

Participant

The single most important role to be assumed by a client system is that of active participant. Too often organizational change gets done to others, rather than being produced by them. Active participation at every organizational level is the foundation for the building blocks of organizational evolution and learning.

Mutual Roles

In addition to the individual roles of change agents and client systems in organizational change, there should be roles which are mutually shared. Without various roles being shared, organizational change becomes an act rather than a process. Among these important roles to be played are problem solver, diagnostician, learner, and monitor.

Problem Solver

Both the change agent and the client system must actively assume the role of problem solver. If both are not actually pursuing the same problem, the investment in actual change becomes greater than the outcome. Only when both parties collaborate to mutually identify problems, define issues, generate alternatives, and test assumptions does the change process realize its potential outcomes.

Diagnostician

The mutual role of diagnostician must be assumed continuously by both parties. Both change agents and client systems should scan the organizational environment for areas of concern that will impair the change effort or block the change goals. Change agents and client systems should also be able to accurately diagnose the nature of the relationship between themselves so that sensitivity to issues surrounding their mutual tasks can be maximized.

Learner

Since many of the experiences in organizational development are situation-specific, it is paramount that both parties assume a learning role. From an organizational perspective, the primary reason for relying upon a change agent is a member's failure to learn and adapt. The primary goal of most organizational interventions is to acquire knowledge, skills, or attitudes which can be generalized to situations facing the organization. Similarly, the role of learner must be assumed by the change agent, despite the other roles of educator/trainer and technical expert. For the change agent, interventions offer the opportunity for much exploration, testing, and refinement of skills. This notion is closely related to Steele's (1967) notion of student.

Monitor

The mutual role of monitor is possibly the most difficult to assume for both the change agent and the client system. The role of monitor involves the mutual responsibility to monitor not only all phases of the change effort, but to monitor the change relationship as well. The task is to remain aware of alternatives, consequences of actions, and the effectiveness of the change effort and relationship at each stage of the intervention. This mutual role is similar to Steele's (1968) change agent role of monitor, but applied here to *collaborative roles* of both parties.

Role Multiplicity

Roles played by change agents and client systems, both singularly and mutually, can be seen as the catalyst for much of the activity in an OD effort. The extent to which these roles are clear and well structured will undoubtedly dictate much of the success or failure in any intervention effort. Figure 4.4 illustrates the variety of roles to be adopted and portrayed in an OD intervention. As shown, each role is a subset of a larger role system. This notion is predicated upon the fact that the adoption of these roles by change agents and client systems does not occur in a vacuum. Rather, each role can be adopted independently as well as simultaneously with other roles, depending entirely upon the requirements of the situation, or stage of change.

Role multiplicity—that is, the extent to which change agents and client systems can adopt various roles—can be seen as a critical element in any intervention. A number of authors (Margulies and Raia, 1972; Lippitt and Lippitt, 1978) have elaborated upon the multiplic-

FIG. 4.4. Roles Portrayed in a Change Effort

ity of consultative roles. Margulies and Raia (1977) divide consultant's roles into task oriented and process oriented roles. Roles with a task orientation require the consultant to act as a technical expert. Roles with a process orientation have the consultant act as a process facilitator. Lippitt and Lippitt (1976) describe consultant roles on a decision-making continuum from directive to nondirective. At the nondirective level, consultants direct the problem-solving process by preparing guidelines and through direct persuasion. On the nondirective end of the continuum, the consultant merely raises questions for reflection. Without question, the skill with which specific roles are adopted under given circumstances, and the cooperative adoption of mutual roles, ultimately structures the nature of the intervention, and its effectiveness.

STAGES OF THE OD PROCESS

Models of Change

Important to the professional practice of any OD practitioner are the stages of change through which an intervention will progress. Of specific importance are the prescriptive roles of change agents and client systems as they move from one major stage to the next. It is with fuller understanding of change stages and specific roles associated with each stage that a technically sound intervention can be implemented and a mature relationship be built for all change parties.

Irrespective of intervention goals, means, or methods, OD efforts engage in phases or stages which dictate all future intervention efforts. Many popular models of the change process have been developed as a function of the techniques used to induce change. For example, people change strategies such as grid development, management by objectives, t-groups, process consultation, survey feedback, team building, etc., have evolved specific techniques for inducing change in people and the way they work together. Most of these techniques, now that they are widely used, have refined the sequence of intervention events which should be followed from beginning to end. This is also true of interventions aimed at an organization's technology, task, or structure (i.e., sociotechnical systems, matrix organization, etc.).

While there is some debate as to whether all the techniques used to change people, structure, tasks, or technology can truly be called

OD, most share one problem. Few popular change models that are associated with a particular change technology simultaneously explain the stages of organizational change, while also illustrating the necessary relationships between the change agent and the client system. Unfortunately, these models do not include all the stages typically involved in organizational change, nor do they fully deal with how roles of the change parties should change at various change stages.

However, a variety of OD theorists have developed pure models of change, irrespective of the various techniques used. Some of these approaches focus more upon stages of global behavior change on the part of organizational participants (Lewin, 1951; Griener, 1967; Lippitt, Wesley, and Watson, 1958), and others have focused more specifically upon the stages of the change agent-client system relationship (Bell and Nadler 1979). Several models have combined many of the major change stages with the stages of the relationship between the client system and the change agent (Lippitt and Lippitt, 1976; Schein, 1969). Table 4.3 illustrates the comparison of the stages involved in organizational change and consultation by the various authors and theorists.

Chronologically, Lewin's (1951) model is considered to be the first model of systems change applicable to OD. Although originally used for analysis of changes in small groups, it is the foundation upon which all others rest. As shown, the three phases are unfreezing, changing, and freezing. After Lewin (1951) a comprehensive model was developed by Lippitt, Watson, and Wesley (1958). This model includes stages integral to an organization-wide change effort. Their seven stages are scouting, entry, diagnosis, planning, action, stabilization and evaluation, and termination. Kolb and Froham (1970) later refined this model, devising an organization development approach to consulting. Kolb and Froham added several feedback loops from planning to entry, and from evaluation to planning, thus illustrating the cyclical nature of an intervention.

Following Lewin (1957) and Lippitt, Watson, and Wesley (1958), Griener (1967) investigated patterns of successful change in a variety of organizations. He concluded that successful OD was a series of six different stimulus-response stages. The stages are pressure and arousal, intervention and reorientation, diagnosis and recognition, invention and commitment, experimentation and search, and reinforcement and acceptance. After Griener (1967), Schein's (1969) stages of pro-

TABLE 4.3. Comparison of Stages Involved in Organization Change and Consultation

Lewin 1951	Lippitt, Watson, and Wesley 1958	Griener 1967	Schein 1967	Bell and Nadler 1979	Lippitt and Lippitt 1976
Unfreezing	Scouting and Entry	Pressure and Arousal	Initial Contact	Entry	Contact and Entry
Changing	Diagnosis, Planning, and Action	Intervention and Relationship	Definition of the Relationship	Diagnosis	Formulating a contract and establishing a helping relationship
		Diagnosis and Recognition	Selecting and setting a method of work	Response	Problem Identification and diagnostic analysis
		Invention and Commitment	Data Gathering and Diagnosis	Disengagement	Goal Setting and Planning
		Experimentation and Search	Intervention	Closure	Taking Action and Cycling Feedback
Freezing	Stabilization, Evaluation, and Termination	Reinforcement and Acceptance	Reducing Involvement		Contract Completion: Continuity, Support, Termination
			Termination		

cess consultation model was popularized. His seven stages of consulting have remained an excellent vehicle to explore change agent-client system issues. The stages include initial contact, definition of the relationship, selecting and setting a method of work, data gathering and diagnosis, intervention, reducing involvement, and termination.

More recently, Lippitt and Lippitt (1976) and Bell and Nadler (1979) have proposed change models, both of which involve themselves heavily with the change agent-client system relationship. Lippitt and Lippitt's (1976) phases in consulting are perhaps the most complete and descriptive of those yet developed. They have developed six stages and five areas of work focus. These six stages are contact and entry, formulating a contract and establishing a helping relationship, problem identification and diagnostic analysis, goal setting and planning, taking action and cycling feedback, and contract completion. Later, Bell and Nadler (1979) developed a five-stage model, depicting the stages in a consulting relationship. These stages are entry, diagnosis, response, disengagement, and closure.

As can be seen, most change models have several common properties. There are typically at least three major phases, although many authors break the major phases down into specific steps or stages. Lewin's (1951) unfreezing step is closely related to Griener's (1967) notion of pressure and arousal, Bell and Nadler's (1979) stage of entry, Lippitt and Lippitt's (1976) notion of contact and entry, Lippitt, Watson, and Wesley's (1958) step of scouting and entry, and Schein's (1969) notion of initial contact and definition of a relationship. Lewin's (1951) stage of unfreezing can also be roughly equated to stages in other models involving the diagnostic process and problem identification.

Lewin's (1951) step of changing can also be roughly compared to the activating stages of an intervention where actual changes in behavior are attempted. For example, Griener's (1967) stages of intervention and commitment and experimentation and search are roughly equated. Bell and Nadler's (1979) stage of response, Lippitt and Lippitt's stage of goal setting and planning, taking action and cycling feedback, Lippitt, Watson and Wesley's (1958) stage of action, and Schein's (1967) stage of intervention are similar. Further Lewin's (1951) notion of freezing is comparable to Griener's (1967) stage of reinforcement and acceptance, Bell and Nadler's (1979) step of disengagement, Lippitt and Lippitt's stage of contract completion, and Lippitt, Watson, and Wesley's (1958) notion of stabilization and evaluation.

An Alternative View of the OD Process

Because of the relatively few well developed and popularly accepted models that include the relationship between the client system and change agent, and the change process itself, a serious deficit has occurred. That is, there has not been a systematic attempt to fully investigate change agent and client system behavior at various stages of change. Figure 4.5 is an attempt to globally illustrate the role episodes that should occur between the change agent and the client system at various stages of an OD effort. This process-relational model illustrates ten stages of OD which deal with the conceptual framework of most organizational change methodologies (i.e., diagnosis, intervention, evaluation, etc.), in addition to focusing on the role relationship between the parties involved (i.e., initiation, clarification, termination, etc.).

FIG. 4.5. A Process Relational Model of Organizational Development

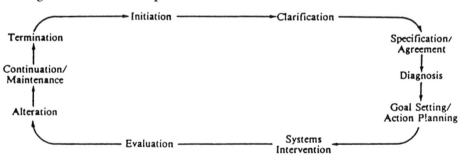

Source: From White, L. P., Wooten, K. C. "Ethical Dilemmas in Various Stages of Organizational Development." *Academy of Management Review* 8, no. 4, 1983, p. 693.

Although this process-relational model is shown to be sequentially cyclical, its sequential appearance is depicted to illustrate what should occur in the ideal form. By their structure and content many organizational change techniques, methodologies, and practices do not systematically deal with one or several of these important stages. Implicit in this model is that these stages typically occur between the client system and the change agent, either consciously or unconsciously. On the conscious level, if each of these ten stages is dealt with and worked through successfully between the client system and change agent, there is a lower probability that ethical breaches will occur.

Implicit also in the process-relational model is the fact that the change agent-client system relationship in any organizational change effort represents a collection of interrelated activities in which both the change agent and the client system play a role in reaching a predetermined course. Using the role system model developed by Katz and Kahn (1968) presented earlier, the behavior, or role behavior, of the change agent and client system during each stage of an organizational change effort can be studied as a role episode, or series of role episodes. As a role episode, the change agent-client system relationship at each stage of an organizational change effort represents a sequence of role sending and role receiving. Thus, Figure 4.5 draws upon models previously developed to integrate the major steps and stages, while at the same time fully illustrating the prescriptive roles for both change agents and client systems at each of these stages.

Initiation

The process-relational model begins at the stage of initiation. This can be considered the initial contact or role episode between the change agent and the client system. This stage, as a behavior setting or role episode, may occur under differing circumstances and on more than one occasion. This initiation stage generally involves the first face to face encounter or meeting. Initiation is the first information sharing on the part of the change agent and the client system. This stage is therefore closely related to Bell and Nadler's (1979) stage of entry, Lippitt and Lippitt's (1976) stage of entry, Lippitt, Watson, and Wesley's (1958) stage of scouting, and Schein's (1969) notion of initial contact. To a lesser extent, initiation is related to Lewin's (1951) notion of unfreezing, and Griener's (1967) notion of pressure and arousal.

In initiation, it is the specific role of the change agent to provide information concerning education, background, expertise, working arrangements, and personal values. The client system needs to provide the change agent with information of its possible needs, history, global problems, and interest of management and representative groups. During initiation the client system must actively portray the role of information supplier while the change agent must actively portray the role of model and technical expert. Mutually, they both must engage in the roles of learner.

Clarification

The next stage illustrated in the model is clarification. This typically involves the second, third, or perhaps up to the fifth or sixth encounter or role episode between the change agent and the client system. The purpose of the clarification stage is for further elaboration of the previous initiation stage. Although quite similar in content to the initiation stage, this stage is typified by "checking out" and "reality testing" of all previous information and data. This stage will typically involve further discussion on the part of the client system of its general culture and internal politics, as well as individual risk and interest. This stage, due to its relatedness to initiation, is similar to the stages of the models mentioned.

As in initiation, a variety of prescriptive roles should be portrayed by both the change agent as well as the client system. In this case it is the role of the client system to make known to the change agent whether or not further discussion of a possible relationship is perceived to be mutually beneficial. The role of the change agent should involve greater discussion about precise education, licensure, experience, operative values, and optimal working conditions. The role on the part of the change agent should involve a further exploration of the client's possible needs, more detailed organizational history, special problems with management, personnel, workforce, marketplace, or government. The change agent should engage in the role of model, and in this case to model honesty and openness concerning skills, needs, intent, etc. The change agent must also portray the role of researcher/theoretician to clarify his/her needs, goals, as well as those of the client system. As was true for initiation, the client system should be an information supplier. Both need to adopt the new role of diagnostician as they clarify and explore the relevant issues shaping their relationship.

Specification/Agreement

The third stage of the process-relational model is specification/agreement. The purpose of this stage is for succinct elaboration of client needs, problems, and interest, as well as the change agent's fees, services, and working conditions. The culmination of this stage should be a mutual agreement as to a working arrangement, possibly under legal contract. Distinct from the first two stages, the specification/agreement stage should include a time frame and an understanding of the conditions under which the relationship would be terminated. This step should also include a mutual agreement as to what resources are to be provided by either party and when, what action steps are to be taken by both parties with a specification of accountability.

As a role episode, or series of role episodes, this stage may occur shortly after initiation and clarification, or it may require sufficient time for decisions to be made by either party. This stage is therefore closely related to Lippitt and Lippitt's (1970) stage of formulating a contract and relationship development, Lippitt, Watson, and Wesley's (1958) stage of entry, and Schein's (1969) definition of the relationship. To a lesser degree it is related to Griener's (1967) stage of pressure and arousal, where an organization, based on stimuli, overtly gains consciousness of its problems and commits to a course of action.

In specification/agreement, the role of the client system is to specify the needs to be addressed, whose needs they are, the subsystems of the organization that an intervention might involve, a possible time frame for activities to occur, and the specification of possible end-state outcomes (i.e., possible goals and objectives, or evaluative criteria). It is the role of the change agent to specify the actual services in terms of actions to be taken, with what parties, what fees would be contingent upon specific system changes or periods of time, and under what conditions the consultant is willing to work, or not work. Thus, the change agent should continue to portray the role of researcher/theoretician, as well as that of technical expert. As for the client system, the roles of information supplier and that of participant appear most appropriate. Both parties should maintain the roles of learner and adopt the role of problem solver to work out many of the difficulties that might arise at this stage.

Diagnosis

The fourth stage in the process-relational model is diagnosis. This is the stage where the change agent first interfaces with members of the client system other than the contracting party. The purpose of this stage is to obtain an unfiltered and undistorted view of problems and actual behaviors or the cultural system and subsystems to be dealt with. It is the purpose of this stage to pinpoint actual change targets and the development of specific change criteria. This stage is therefore closely related to stages in many other models of change. This stage is related to Griener's (1967) stage of diagnosis and recognition, Lippitt and Lippitt's (1976) stage of problem identification and diagnostic analysis, as well as Schein's (1969) stage of data gathering and diagnosis.

In the stage of diagnosis the specific role of the client system is to assist the change agent in collecting the needed data. This stage is typified by such actions as interviewing system members, unobtrusive observation, process observation, role analysis, sociometry, personnel or product/service research, or survey research. The role of the change agent in diagnosis is to collect data concerning the organization's problems, analyze and feed back these data to organizational members. The change agent's specific role at this stage is technical expert and researcher/theoretician. The client system should assume the four specific roles of resource provider, supporter/advocate, information supplier, and especially that of participant. Both change parties should assume the roles of problem solver, diagnostician, and learner.

Goal Setting/Action Planning

The fifth stage is goal setting/action planning. The purpose of this stage is to establish the specific goals to be achieved by an intervention. It is the purpose of this stage to develop strategies concerning what should be done in terms of change activities, how it will be done, when it will be done, who will be responsible and accountable for it, what resources will be necessary, and how specific goals will be measured to determine effectiveness. This stage is distinct from the previous stage, in that it clarifies a specific change goal, whereas the stage of diagnosis pinpoints change targets and develops the initial change criteria. It is most closely related to Lippitt and Lippitt's

(1976) stage of goal setting and planning, Schein's (1969) stage of selecting and setting a method of work, and Griener's (1967) stage of intervention and commitment.

In the stage of goal setting/action planning, the specific role of both the change agent and client system is to mutually set achievable goals which address the organization's problems, and agree upon change strategies that can adequately address the needs of the organization. The change agent should engage in the role of technical expert, based on his/her expertise and knowledge from previous interventions. The change agent should also engage the role of theoretician to work with the client in building a conceptual model of what should follow in the intervention. The client should actively engage in the roles of participant, as well as resource provider and supporter/advocate to make the OD intervention a process as opposed to an act. Both change parties should actively engage in the role of problem solver, hopefully by creatively determining together the methods and means to help the organization and its members grow and adapt.

Systems Intervention

Systems intervention is the sixth stage in the model. The purpose of this stage is to begin the actual intervention into the ongoing behavior, structure, or processes of the social system, based on the results of the diagnosis intervention. Systems intervention is similar to the stage of diagnosis in that it includes an interface between the change agent and the members of the client system. It is different, however, with respect to actions aimed at change, as opposed to data gathering and development of specific goals, objectives, and strategies. This stage is similar to Lewin's (1951) notion of changing. It is also closely related to Bell and Nadler's (1979) stage of response, Lippitt and Lippitt's (1976), Lippitt, Watson, and Wesley's (1958) stage of taking action, and Schein's (1969) stage of intervention.

During this stage, it is the role of the change agent to begin intervening in the social system, at specific targeted changes and at a specific depth of intervention. Concurrently, it is the specific role of the client system to invest the energy and resources required by planned intervention. The change agent must assume the role of technical expert, using specific techniques, and as an educator/trainer if the intervention requires such. The change agent frequently must link the client system to needed internal or external resources. If the intervention requires aquisition of behavioral skills, the change agent must act as a model as well. On the other hand the client system must remain a strong resource provider, supporter/advocate, and a participant. It is critical that both parties actively assume the role of learner, as new behaviors, strategies, and processes are tried out.

Evaluation

The seventh stage of the process-relational model is evaluation. The purpose of the evaluation stage is to measure changes that occur in the agreed upon change criteria over a specific period of time. The implicit purpose is to make a determination of the effectiveness of the social intervention, the actions and strategies of the change agent and the energy and resources utilized by the client system. Thus, the purpose of evaluation is to determine the quality of the intervention, as well as the relationship propelling it. This stage is similiar to that of diagnosis, in that some form of effort to collect objective data concerning the organization and its effectiveness should be made. The evaluation stage is directly comparable to Lippitt and Lippitt's (1976) notion of cycling feedback, and Lippitt, Watson, and Wesley's (1958) stage of stabilization and evaluation.

In evaluation, it is the specific role of the change agent to gather data on specified targets of change, and report or present these data to the client system; and to analyze the evaluation data and determine its effectiveness. Both the client system and change agent must determine the effectiveness of not only the social intervention but of the relationship between them and determine how and when the relationship should follow. The change agent must maintain the role of technical expert from the previous stage, as well as assume the role of researcher/theoretician. The client system must maintain the role of resource provider and participant, and again assume the information supplier role. Both must maintain the roles of learner, diagnostician, and monitor, to a greater degree.

Alteration

Alteration constitutes the eighth stage of the process-relational model. The purpose of alteration is the needed modification of change strategy, depth or level of intervention; change goals, resources to be utilized, or time frame, etc., as deemed appropriate by both the change agent and the client system.

Alteration then differs from the three previous stages, and more closely resembles the stages of initiation, clarification, and specification/agreement. Here the change agent is not making an actual intervention into the social system, rather the change agent and the client system are focusing on the clarification and specification of a continuing relationship. Typical activities in this stage revolve around the nature of the data (i.e., negative, positive, or neutral) that are presented to the client system during evaluation. At this stage, one or all of the next three stages may occur (i.e., alteration, continuation/maintenance, or termination). This seventh stage then is obviously closely related to the stage of diagnosis intervention. Alteration is comparable only to Lippitt and Lippitt's (1976) stage of contract completion where continuity is provided after the actual intervention.

Alterations must be made by the change agent if necessary to meet the original change goal/target, or to offer a new change goal and the strategies necessary to achieve it, based on the evaluation intervention. Needs and expectations of the client system must be made known to provide the context for a redefinition of the original agreement between the two parties if necessary. The change agent maintains the role of technical expert and researcher/theoretician, and more frequently needs to assume the role of resource linker. The client system should maintain all four roles of participant, resource provider, supporter/advocate, and information supplier. Both parties' most important mutual roles to be assumed are those of problem solver and diagnostician.

Continuation/Maintenance

Figure 4.5 indicates that the ninth stage in the process-relational model is continuation/maintenance. The purpose of this stage is twofold. First, its purpose is to monitor and maintain the ongoing change strategies initiated by the systems intervention, and provide periodical checks on progress based on the change criteria developed in goal setting/action planning or alteration. The second purpose is to continue a social intervention based on altered change goals, targets, change criteria, and change strategies, which can be typified by repeating the stages of systems intervention and evaluation. Continuation/maintenance then, closely resembles the actions of systems intervention. This stage is closely related to Griener's (1967) stage of reinforcement and acceptance, as well as Lippitt and Lippitt's (1976) stage of contract completion where continued support is rendered.

In continuation/maintenance it is the role of the change agent to make sure that an ongoing intervention resides within the strategy of the original intervention, at the same depth, with the same target, or specified alternatives as agreed upon in the stage of alteration. Parameters of the continuation and maintenance of the relationship must be specified (i.e., time frame, how the relationship may change in the future, and the resources that will be required).

The specific role of the client system is to provide or allocate the resources or energy required to maintain or continue the intervention. The change agent should again assume the role of model and educator/trainer if required, while maintaining the role of technical expert. The client system must as well maintain the roles of resource provider, supporter/advocate, and participant. Both must assume and maintain the roles of monitor and learner.

Termination

The tenth and final stage in the process-relational model is termination. The purpose of this stage is to establish a monitoring system to allow for long term determination of effectiveness of the change effort and to turn over the change process entirely to the client system. As for the change agent disengaging from the client system, there are three typical reasons. The first reason for termination is that the change goals and targets have been met, and the client system has the necessary adaptive processes internally to continue or maintain the change or a level of change. Second, the change agent leaves the change effort based on unfulfilled contractual agreements, lack of change through agreed upon criteria, or unethical behavior from the perspective of the client system. Third, the change agent may leave the change effort because contractual needs could be better met by another party. This stage is closely related to Bell and Nadler's (1979) steps of disengagement and closure, Lippitt and Lippitt's (1976) notion of contract completion where termination is the focus, and the stage of termination as proposed by Lippitt, Watson, and Wesley (1958) and Schein (1969).

The specific role of the change agent in the tenth stage is to disengage services based on one of the actions discussed above. The specific role of the client system is to fulfill their role as detailed in the stages of specification/agreement, alteration, or continuation/maintenance, and to evaluate the overall effectiveness of the intervention for eventual feedback to the change agent and organizational members. The client system must also determine its stage of organizational health, and whether it has developed adaptive processes congruent with its original needs. Thus, the role best portrayed by the change agent at this stage is researcher/theoretician, and that of resource linker. All four roles of resource provider, supporter/advocate, information supplier, and participant must be portrayed by the client system. The mutual role most critical at this stage is one of monitor.

SUMMARY

This chapter has explored both the specific roles of change agents and the stages of change that an OD effort progresses through. Starting with an acceptable framework for analyzing change agent-client system behavior, this framework was applied to general and specific roles at various stages of change. Use of Katz and Kahn's (1966) role episodic model allows for investigation of each client system-change agent interaction as a role episode, or behavior setting, and a role sending sequence. These role episodes have role senders and role receivers portrayed interchangably by the change parties. From these role episodes, and the factors which influence them, illustration can be given to forms of role conflict and role overload which significantly influences the interventions' effectiveness and modifies the change relationship. It can be shown that through role sending and role receiving that intersender conflict, intrasender conflict, interrole conflict, person-role conflict and role overload can frequently occur.

A model (Fig. 4.3) illustrating the impact of various roles upon the effectiveness of OD was built upon the expanded Katz and Kahn (1966) role episode model. From this model, it can be shown that the role of the change agent and the client system is greatly modified by the personal values, goals, skills/abilities, needs, and resources, as well as the internal and external organizational climate. These in turn are influenced by, and influence, the goals, strategies, and targets of the OD effort, as well as the interventions' means and methods. A causal model can therefore be used for exploring the efforts of change roles in any intervention.

Literature concerning roles of change agents and client systems was critically reviewed and compared, indicating much similarity in philosophy and approach. From such, basic roles for change agents, basic roles for client systems, and mutual roles can be offered. Roles such as resource provider, technical expert, researcher/theoretician, model, and educator/trainer appear appropriate for change agents. Roles such as resources provider, supporter/advocate, information supplier, and participant are suggested for client systems. Mutual roles of problem solver, diagnostician, learner, and monitor seem plausible for both change parties. Role multiplicity, defined as situationally appropriate adoption of change roles, can be viewed from its overall contribution to OD success.

Literature involving stages of change in OD and phases of the consulting process were critically reviewed and compared. From a comparative analysis a process-relational model that integrates stages of change and phases of a change agent-client system relationship was offered. Ten specific stages of change were depicted, comparing each to previous models. Change stages of initiation, clarification, specification/agreement, diagnosis, goal setting/action planning, systems intervention, evaluation, alternation, continuation/maintenance, and termination are suggested, illustrating specific goals and behaviors at each stage. Specific roles to be played by both change agents and client systems at these various stages can be analyzed, thereby illustrating the dynamic nature of planned change.

NOTES

Argyris, C. *Intervention Theory and Method: A Behavioral Science View.* Reading, Mass.: Addison-Wesley, 1970.

Bell, C. R. and Nadler, L. (eds.). *The Client-Consultant Handbook.* Houston, Tex.: Gulf Publishing Company, 1979.

Bennis, W. C. "Theory and Method in Applying Behavioral Science to Planned Organizational Change." In A. Bartlett and T. Kayser, *Changing Organizational Behavior.* Englewood Cliffs, N.J.: Prentice-Hall, 1973, 63–75.

Bernadin, H. "The Predictability of Discrepancy Measures of Role Constructs." *Journal of Applied Psychology* 32, no. 1, 1979, 39–153.

Blake, R. R. and Mouton, J. S. *Consultation.* Reading, Mass.: Addison-Wesley, 1976.

Griener, L. E. "Patterns of Organizational Change." *Harvard Business Review* 45, 1967, 119-28.

Havelock, R. G. *The Change Agents Guide to Innovation in Education.* Englewood Cliffs, N.J.: Educational Technology Publications, 1973.

House, R. J. and Rizzo, R. J. "Role Conflict and Ambiguity as Critical Variables in a Model of Organizational Behavior." *Organizational Behavior and Human Performance* 7, 1972, 467-505.

Kahn, R. N., Wolfe, D. M., Quinn, R. P., Snoek, J. D., and Rosenthal, R. A. *Organizational Stress: Studies in Role Conflict and Ambiguity.* New York: Wiley, 1964.

Katz, D. and Kahn, R. L. *The Social Psychology of Organizations.* New York: John Wiley and Sons, 1966.

Kolb, D. A. and Fronham, A. L. "An Organization Development Approach to Consulting." *Sloan Management Review* 12, no. 1, 1970, 51-65.

Lawrence, P. R. and Lorsch, J. D. *Developing Organizations: Diagnosis and Action.* Reading, Mass.: Addison-Wesley, 1969.

Lewin, K. *Field Theory in Social Science.* New York: McGraw-Hill, 1951.

Lippitt, G. L. and Lippitt, R. *The Consultant Process in Action.* La Jolla, Col.: University Associates, 1978.

Lippitt, R., Watson, J. and Westley, B. *The Dynamics of Planned Change*, New York: Harcourt, Brace, and World, 1958.

Margulies, N. and Raia, A. *Organizational Development: Values, Process, and Technology.* New York: McGraw-Hill, 1972.

Menzel, R. K. "A Taxonomy of Change Agent Skills." *Journal of European Training* 4, no. 5, 1975, 287-88.

Mirvis, P. H., and Seashore, S. E. "Being Ethical in Organizational Research." *American Psychologist* 34, no. 9, 1979, 766-80.

Nadler, L. *Developing Human Resources.* Houston, Tex.: Gulf Publishing, 1980.

Rizzo, J. R., House, R. J. and Lietzman, S. I. "Role Conflict and Ambiguity in Complex Organizations." *Administrative Science Quarterly* 15, 1970, 150–63.

Sashkin, M. "Models and Roles of Change Agents." In J. W. Pfeiffer and J. E. Jones (eds.). *The 1974 Handbook for Group Facilitators.* La Jolla, Cal.: University Associates, 1974.

Schein, E. H. *Process Consultation: Its Role in Organization Development.* Reading, Mass.: Addison-Wesley, 1969.

Steele, F. *Consulting for Organizational Change.* Amherst, Mass.: University of Massachusetts Press, 1975.

Szilagyi, A. D., Sims, H. D., Jr., and Keller, R. T. "Role Dynamics, Locus of Control, and Employee Attitudes and Behavior." *Academy of Management Journal* 19, 1976, 219-76.

Tracy, L. and Johnson, T. W. "What do the Role Conflict and Role Ambiguity Scales Measure?" *Journal of Applied Psychology* 66, 1981, 464-69.

White, L. P. and Wooten, K. C. "Ethical Dilemmas in Various Stages of Organizational Development." *Academy of Management Review* 8, no. 4, 1983, 690-97.

Wooten, K. C. and White, L. P. "Ethical Problems in the Practice of Organizational Development." *Training and Development Journal* 37, no. 4, 1983, 16-25.

5

The Client-Consultant Relationship

INTRODUCTION

While many of the problems facing organizations today are technological in nature, and therefore not fully amenable to the use of behavioral science techniques, it is the human element that by and large tends to produce success or failure in today's organizational change activities. Specifically, it is the human element and relationship between the change agent and the client system which frequently tend to inhibit or propel the change progress in OD. While some authors suggest that readiness to change (Griener, 1967), or appropriateness of the change technology (Bowers, 1973; Porras, 1978) are the paramount variables in the change effort, it is reasonable to assume that the relationship between the change agent and the client system is of equal if not primary importance.

It is becoming increasingly clear that successful change agent-client system relationships are those in which both the change agent and the client system adopt the appropriate roles and constantly strive toward a mature relationship. Therefore, the high cost of failure in OD necessitates that maximum effort be placed on developing a mature and rewarding change relationship. Concerning unsuccessful OD efforts, Ford (1974) notes "in very simple terms in those cases which did not work out, either the consultant did not do what he should have, or the client did not do what he should have done. More likely, the answer lies in a combination of mutual adaptability" (p. 3).

The obvious need for all OD theorists, practitioners, and consumers revolves around the question of how to achieve and maintain a mature change relationship. Underlying this question is the exploration of what factors influence the change relationship, the issues frequently encountered, and the consequences of a mature change relationship. The strategies useful in achieving change maturity is equally important.

THE NATURE OF THE CHANGE RELATIONSHIP

Factors Influencing the Change Relationship

Many authors have written extensively about the nature of the relationship between the change agent and the client system. Reviews have ranged from the development of a relationship (Ford, 1974; Kaplan, 1978), the nature of the OD contract (Milstein & Smith, 1979; Weisbord, 1973), to the depth of the intervention itself (Harrison, 1970). Other works have involved the unshifting and manipulative properties that potentially can occur in a change relationship. Contemporary OD text by French & Bell (1976), Huse (1980), and Lippitt (1982), also deal with the change relationship between client and consultant.

Irrespective of the many approaches, issues, and areas explored in the relational properties between the client system and the change agent, it appears that what occurs is endemic to any relationship generally, and to the helping relationship specifically. What is not entirely clear is how specific issues and factors combine to produce unique relationships between change parties.

Lippitt and Lippitt (1978), describe the dynamic nature of the relationship between the change agent and client system as follows:

> Each step of the process of consulting confronts the helper and the client with a series of interaction decisions and possible alternatives for behavioral strategy. These interaction decisions and behaviors primarily may be the response of a would-be helper to the expressions of need, concern, from a client (person or group), or they may be initiated by the helper to stimulate a desire for help, to establish a helping contact, and activate problem solving efforts on the part of the client. . . . These interactions may be part of the informal process of give and take between peers—a voluntary process of friendship; a more deliberative

effort of a parent, or older friend, or a more experienced person to give help on a problem; or the efforts of a professional helper. (p. 8)

Similarly, Bennis describes the integral nature of the change agent-client system relationship. He states:

> Acceptance (of change) also depends on the relationship between the change agent and the client system. The more profound and anxiety producing the change, the more collaborative and close relationship is required. In addition, we can predict that an anticipated change will be resisted to the degree that the client system possesses little or incorrect knowledge about the change, have relatively little trust in the source of change, and have relatively low influence in controlling the nature and the definition of change. (p. 175)

Given all the properties that can be observed in the OD relationship, what then are the major factors which influence it? There are essentially five factors which influence the roles played by the change agent and the client system, and the subsequent effectiveness of the OD effort. These factors are values, goals, needs, skills/abilities, and resources (Fig. 5.1).

FIG. 5.1. Factors Influencing the Change Agent-Client System Relationship

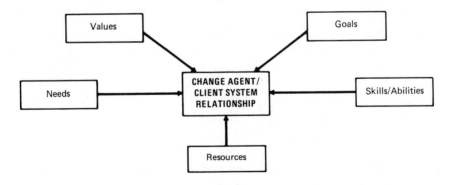

Values

Without question, the values to be optimized or changed is an inherent aspect of the OD process itself. In some interventions, a change of values may in fact be the target of the intervention entirely. The factor of values influences whether or not an organization engages in OD. The decision to do OD in military organizations places the values of those involved under considerable strain (Huse, 1980). Results such as participatory leadership, optimum utilization of the human resources, and increased satisfaction and productivity are all the result of optimizing the values of the change agent and the client system, to a greater or lesser degree.

Recent works (Friedlander and Brown, 1974; Alderfer, 1977), (Margulies and Raia, 1972) have strongly stressed the importance of values. Friedlander and Brown (1977) noted that "the future of OD rests in part on its values and the degree to which its practices, theory and research are congruent with its values" (p. 335). Such relatedness between values, beliefs, and practices have been well documented by Tichy (1974). Values of change agents and client systems are rarely the same, however, and in some cases are in direct opposition to one another. Value dilemmas, then, are frequently encountered in consulting (Bowen, 1977). The working through and exploration of these many value differences will allow the OD process to flourish.

Needs

Another characteristic or factor in the change agent-client system relationship is needs, and complex needs networks. Each parties' needs may range from an impersonal perspective to a personal perspective. In this sense, a broad range of needs, many of which are conflicting may be present in an OD relationship. To compound the situation further, needs will change substantially as the change effort progresses from one need to the next.

It is reasonable to suggest that no true OD effort will meet everyone's needs to the fullest, nor should it. When OD is done well, there are typically numerous efforts at collaborating towards a common goal. To reach a common goal, it may be necessary to satisfy some needs of the change agent or the client system to achieve the more global needs of system-wide change.

From the client systems perspective, Bennis (1969) notes "that organizational development is necessary whenever our social institutions compete for survival under conditions of chronic change" (p. 19). Rapid and unexpected change, growth in size, increasing diversity, and required changes in managerial behavior are typical needs being frequently expressed by nearly all contemporary organizations (Bennis, 1969). It is reasonable to expect that organizations in the 1980s and 1990s will have more complex and salient needs. As the world becomes more deficient of needed resources, and more dependent upon large organizations, the client systems needs in OD will obviously broaden.

Change agents as well have complex needs, e.g., the need to grow interpersonally and professionally, and the need to learn from experience. Interestingly, needs of the change agent such as performing professionally, earning a reasonable wage, and receiving professional esteem from colleagues will in many cases conflict with the client system's need for low-cost solutions, minimal disruption in organizational structure and process, and low risk of labor unrest.

Goals

Similar to the influence of needs on the change agent and the client system is the influence of goals upon the change relationship. Again, both change agents and client systems may have differing goals. Goals of both the change agent and the client system are linked to the values and needs surrounding the change relationship. Most OD efforts typically have operational goals such as helping the client system become more self-renewing, to optimize effectiveness, move toward high collaboration and low internal competition, improved conflict management, and information/knowledge based decision making (Beckhard, 1969). Similarly, trust, confrontation of problems, knowledge and skill based authority, increased satisfaction creativity, and increased responsibility for planning are frequently focused goals for clients (French, 1969).

Goals on the part of the change agent should be to serve the client to the best of his ability. Idealistically, the goal of the change agent should be to assist the organization to develop and grow to the point where consultant services are no longer needed. Goals like needs and values, however are rarely in any change effort going to exist without conflict and eventual transition as the change relationship progresses.

Skills

Another factor greatly influencing the change relationship is the skill base and abilities of the change agent. Menzel (1975), Lippitt and Lippitt (1978), and Warwick and Donovan (1979), who note that any "list of the professional abilities of a consultant is extensive—something like a combination of the Boy Scout's Laws, requirements for admission to heaven, and the essential elements for securing tenure in an Ivy league school" (p. 355). Similarly Warwick and Donovan (1979) in discussing a survey of OD skills state that "We would like to observe that the skills identified in the survey might be more fitting for superwomen and supermen than for such mortals as OD Practitioners" (p. 25). Warwick and Donovan's (1979) 440 major skills, Menzel's (1975) list of 30 skills and Lippitt and Lippitt's list of 22 competencies are illustrations. Thus, the skills and abilities of the change agent to properly disapprove, intervene, evaluate, and manage an OD effort play a key role in the development of the change relationship.

Equally important to the success of the change relationship are the skills and abilities of the client system. The client system's ability to respond to the change effort and assimilate new skills and values are paramount to the results of the change effort. Within the context of the change relationship, client system and change agent's communication skills and working relationship act frequently as a prerequisite if the skills and competencies of a consultant are to be effective. The goal of much of OD is to transfer skills and abilities of the consultant to the client system problem areas.

Resources

Resources available to both the change agent and client system are equally important factors in the nature of the change relationship. From the perspective of the change agent, resources such as knowledge, expertise, and ties to external persons and institutions are important. If any of these resources are unskillfully used or inappropriately withheld, then the change effort may be placed in jeopardy. The client system also possesses resources integral to the change relationship and exerts considerable influence. Resources such as information, money, time, and commitment of individual client system members and subsystems often hold the key to effective change. The extent to which these resources are available and optimally utilized dictates not only the nature of the change relationship, but the effectiveness of the intervention itself.

Issues in the Change Relationship

As previously noted, issues have been illustrated by many authors concerning the many problems faced by the change agent and the client system. Improper handling of such issues will impair the effectiveness of the change relationship. French and Bell (1976) state that "a number of interrelated issues can occur in a consultant-client relationship in organizational development activity that needs to be managed appropriately if adverse effects are to be overlooked" (p. 171). A review of the literature indicates that there are seven major issues in the change relationship. These issues are trust, dependency, termination and withholding services, appropriateness of intervention means, the contract, determination of the client's identity, and depth and scope of the intervention.

Trust

The issue of trust will at some point or another be a major issue in any OD activity. Not only is trust an essential factor in any effective interpersonal relationship, trust per se may be the motivating force and goal. Interestingly, of the many typical objectives of OD programs, trust and support is one of the most important (French, 1969). During the entry phase of the intervention, it assumes major importance.

The trust issue exists on two levels. The first is interpersonal, the second technical. Frequently operative on both levels is suspicion and mistrust between the change agent and the client system. In dealing with the trust issue, French and Bell (1976) note that the client is often fearful that the organizational system will be totally changed by the interventionist, and his/her techniques. From the perspective of the change agent, they find the consultants' early mistrust revolves around determining the clients' real motives. Lippitt (1982) has hypothesized that this early mistrust in a consulting relationship often results from both parties feeling helpless. Argyris (1970) has found that perceptual client mistrust often may occur. He notes that "clients will tend to defend themselves by selecting behaviors and values that maintain their present level of self-acceptance" (p. 133).

The second level of mistrust exists in the technical realm. Here, clients may mistrust the skills and abilities of the consultant. French and Bell (1971) note that this is a common occurrence in a consulting relationship, and that it generally results from inadequate sharing of assumption, theory, and change technology. So too, there are times change agents mistrust the client's use of a new technology. This is especially true when a change agent does not trust the client system enough to provide sensitive data, knowing that the data would be used to harm organizational members.

Dependency

The second issue, dependency, also frequently occurs in the change relationship. Most change agents have a timetable for reducing the client's dependence upon them. This issue is theoretically and philosophically a difficult one. In some respects, the dependency issue is as much a result of the type of intervention employed by the change agents, as of the abilities of the client system to learn and adapt. Some interventions are, by their very nature, less reliant upon the skills and expertise of the change agent, and therefore not affected by this issue. This is especially true when the change parties can work out a facilitative versus expert role for the change agent (French and Bell, 1976).

The real difficulty of client dependency has more to do with the nature of the helping relationship than the choice of intervention means and roles. Many authors have noted that the change agent-client system relationship, by its very nature, creates dependency. Huse (1980) states that "those who need help are dependent upon the helper. The client can either be counterdependent or overdependent, especially in the early client-consultant relationship" (p. 149).

Termination

An issue very closely related to dependency is termination of the relationship and the withholding of services. This issue is also involved with the values of the change agent, and more importantly, the values of the client system. If the real goal of an intervention is to assist the client to the point where they can adapt, learn, and manage appropriately then termination is a natural occurrence. It is when actions on the part of the client system require the change agent to make a conscious evaluation and ethical judgement concerning where in the change process he/she should terminate the relationship, or perhaps withhold services entirely.

There are two key points in terminating a change relationship. First, there is the issue of whether or not the change agent has a responsibility to the client, irrespective of client values, intentions, or motives, since change will occur with or without the change agent. This is a major difficulty, if the organization may not in the eyes of the change agent be in society's best interest; i.e., military organization, deviant groups, etc. Argyris (1961), maintains that consultants have the same responsibility to their clients as do doctors or lawyers to their clients. Argyris (1970) notes further that free choice is a basic responsibility of both the client and the interventionist, and therefore the consultant has a professional obligation to consider termination when the change relationship is not an effective one.

The second key issue in withholding services and termination is the issue of when to leave. Irrespective of values held by the client, when is it appropriate to leave, given the organization's present level of competence to manage its own learning and change? Assuming that a client's expertise depends upon the effective use of an OD intervention, the decision to leave early becomes all the more difficult. The change agent has an unusual dilemma to resolve if the client system is highly dependent, or in danger of failure, yet there are value differences between change parties. In addressing this problem, Lippitt (1982) maintains that "a special effort is sometimes made to build into the permanent structure of the organizational system a substitute for the renewal facilitation" (p. 74). New procedures, training programs, or new interventions are examples of such efforts.

The Contract

The issue of the contract has long been a major focus for OD practitioners. There are in most cases two forms of contracts in any given intervention. There are both formal and psychological contracts (French and Bell, 1979; Schein, 1969). Formal contracts are those which deal with time, money, space, operational procedures, and the like. The psychological contract on the other hand, is more of an informal agreement that defines the nature of the contract. Both formal and informal contracts are essential to any intervention, and both deal directly with the expectations of the change agent and client system. In many respects, the contract, formal or informal, is used by all parties to specify the characteristics of the relationship.

Concerning the formal contract, a number of ground rules and guidelines are frequently followed although there is no set procedure. Contracts in the consulting field are becoming all the more explicit. The reason for this increasing legitimization is so that both the change agent and the client system can be clear about what to expect (Blake and Mouton, 1976). Effective formal contracts clarify for the consultant three specific areas: (1) what each expects to get from the relationship; (2) how much time each will require, when, and at what cost; and (3) the ground rules under which the parties will operate (Weisbord, 1973). Schein (1973) attempted to clarify the consultant's role by discussing expectations involving proper diagnosis, data gathering, organizational commitment, and most importantly, what he is not willing to do.

Missing from most formal contracts is what to do when factors influencing the relationship necessitate a change in the contract. If one of the most salient characteristics of OD is to learn how to manage change, then being bound by a very rigid contract can have its disdavantages. In addition to general goals, time frame, consultant and client responsibilities, the consultant's boundaries, and arrangements for periodic review and evaluation of the relationship may be contracted for (Gallessich, 1982). Milstein and Smith (1979), exploring such difficulties in a case study, conclude that built-in flexibility in the contract is essential. They state that "OD consultants who are sensitive to the shifting nature of the intervention will probably have to clarify their own values about their role in such efforts" (p. 191).

Client Identification

Determination of who the client is may be an issue throughout any OD intervention. It is perhaps one of the more difficult and dynamic issues to be dealt with. The issue is complex due to the operationalizing of the term "client" in a change agent's system of thinking. The issue is whether the single contracting manager, a specific work group in which the intervention will take place, the entire organization or society in general is the client. As noted by Huse (1980) most OD consultants consider the entire social system to be their client, as opposed to the individual contracting party.

In considering who the client is, both the change agent and the client system are continuously confronted by many decisions. From the perspective of the change agent, the difficulty is frequently one in which the consultant works with only a subsystem of the total organization (French & Bell, 1973; Blake & Mouton, 1980). Often, the dilemma of who the client is results in the change agent losing potency with at least some subsystems in the organization—the subsystem not perceived as the client. Effective consulting, however, involves a relationship between the consultant and all those within the system (French and Bell, 1973).

Determination of who the client is also becomes a difficult issue for the client system for many of the same reasons. If a change agent is more responsive to the broad wishes or needs of the organization rather than the hiring party, conflict is inevitable. Additionally, if the change agent deals only with one group or individual as opposed to the total system, problems will occur. This type of problem is especially likely to occur in multifaceted and multilevel interventions where the composition of the "client" may and should change over time. As interventions progress, client identification is an issue throughout the intervention process (Blake and Mouton, 1980).

Appropriateness of Means

The issue of intervention means and methods can be one of the more difficult issues on the change agent-client system relationship. All change agents, irrespective of background and theoretical alignments, have preferences for specific techniques. Tichy (1973), for example, has shown that the interventionist goals and techniques are closely related to the change agent's values. Change agents, like all human beings, tend to do the things that are more comfortable. There is often the problem of consultants employing techniques that they found successful in the past, irrespective of what may be required. Any intervention method no matter what kind, will prove ineffective if used exclusively (Blake and Mouton, 1980).

Employing appropriate intervention methods is directly tied to the diagnosis process. If the diagnosis is not thorough, or perhaps does not include all system members, the obvious problem of an inappropriate intervention will occur. Moreover, many times the change agent is faced with a predetermined diagnosis upon entry into the organization. Unless the change agent has the freedom to conduct the diagnosis, as well as choose the methods to help the organization, a less than effective effort will occur. Unfortunately, many times clients will force a diagnostic framework upon the change agent, and will insist that certain methods be used. In either case, both the change agent and the client system will not prosper from such pressures. With recent advances in diagnostic methods, as well as more intergrated approaches to intervention, this issue will to some measure become more dynamic.

Depth and Level of the Intervention

Similar to the issue of appropriateness of intervention means is the issue of intervention depth and scope. Its relatedness to the diagnostic process is well noted (Huse, 1980; French & Bell, 1973). This issue is also closely related to the issue of the contract, as well as the determination of the client. Further, a change agent's decisions concerning the depth and scope of an intervention are in large measure a result of their values, as well as skills and abilities. Depth typically refers to resolution of who the change target is. Two fundamental aspects must be addressed when approaching the issue of intervention level (Huse, 1980). This level depends upon both the awareness of the client system and the willingness to take part and upon the personal norms and values of the change agent.

Determination of the appropriate depth in an intervention requires careful diagnosis to determine not only what the problems are, but whose problems they are. Unless both are sufficiently approached, the effect of the intervention will either fall short, or perhaps solve the wrong person's problems. Thus, the problem for the change agent is to determine whether the individual, the group or subgroups, or the formal organizational system should be involved. Additionally, there is the question of what behaviors of the target group should be approached. Interpersonal variables will, in most cases, require greater depth than those involving structure. If an intervention involves structure, technology, and interpersonal variables, the depth and level becomes an issue of maximum importance.

In choosing the appropriate depth, both Harrison (1970) as well as Huse (1980) have developed some guidelines. The level chosen in any intervention must not only be appropriate to a given problem, but should also address the potential climate and readiness to change (Huse, 1980). Harrison (1970) suggests that the dilemma for the change agent is whether to lead or to push to a greater depth. He suggests that change agents should consider the following guidelines:

First, to intervene at a level no deeper than is required to produce en-during solutions to a problem at hand, and second, to intervene at a level no deeper than that at which the energy and resources of the client can be committed to problem solving and change. (p. 201)

THE MATURE CHANGE RELATIONSHIP

Change Agent-Client System Maturity

It could be argued that the relationship between the change agent and the client system is a prime predictor of change effectiveness. To achieve change maturity some essential questions have to be answered. These are: what elements constitute a mature relationship between change parties; and perhaps more importantly, what are the conse-quences of achieving change maturity.

The mature change relationship can be defined and operational-ized from as many different perspectives as there are change relation-ships. It could be argued that each should have its own operational definition of relationship maturity. To conceptualize change ma-turity, however, the mature change agent-client system relationship is one which both parties fulfill their change roles to the fullest, while at the same time meeting the goals of the change intervention. Thus, at whatever stage of change, investigating the mature change relation-ship is one in which all parties are attempting to fulfill their roles, the role expectations of other parties, and manage the factors that influence their relationship.

The mature change relationship focuses on two important varia-bles. The variables are involved with relationship behavior and task behavior. Beginning with Bales (1950) research, and subsequent find-ings referred to as "interaction process analysis," the factors of rela-tionship and task are predominant in literature involving interper-sonal relations. It is interesting to note that most widely accepted models of leadership such as the managerial grid (Blake and Mouton, 1964) the Ohio State Studies (Korman, 1966; Stogdill and Koons, 1957), and the Michigan State Studies (Likert, 1961) all rest on these two important concerns. Contemporary leadership theory (Hersey and Blanchard, 1977) also has primary roots in behaviors concerning the relationship and behaviors concerning the task.

Figure 5.2 depicts relationship behaviors and task behaviors as they relate to the mature change relationship in OD. As shown, there

FIG. 5.2. Maturity Matrix of the Change Relationship

MATURE

MODERATE: Task clarity and specificity MODERATE: Role clarity and flexibility 3	HIGH: Task clarity and specificity HIGH: Role clarity and felxibility 4
1 NO: Task clarity and specificity NO: Role clarity and flexibility	2 LITTLE: Task clarity and specificity LITTLE: Role clarity and flexibility

IMMATURE

are four cells in the maturity matrix. Each cell has components of task clarity (specificity, and components of role clarity) and flexibility. Task clarity and specificity deal with the behaviors in a change relationship having to do with task or goals of the change effort. When the task is clear, a shared conceptualization of what is to be accomplished in a change effort has taken place. When the task has specificity, there is a shared conceptualization of how the task is to be accomplished, that is techniques, methods, and procedures are understood.

Role clarity and role flexibility have to do with the idea of relationship concerns. When the role is clear, there is a shared conceptualization of the appropriateness of assuming different roles when the change effort requires such. When components of the maturity matrix are taken together (Fig. 5.2), they constitute either an immature change relationship or a mature one.

In the first cell of the maturity matrix, an immature relationship is one in which there is little or no task clarity/specificity, or role clarity/flexibility. In the fourth cell, a mature change relationship is depicted. Here, there is an extremely high degree of task clarity and specificity as well as a high degree of role clarity and flexibility.

An immature change relationship exists when what is to be accomplished by the change effort and how this change is to be produced is in question. In the most immature change relationships, no shared conceptualization is present concerning the task to be done. The variables of change, human, structural, or technological will be unclear. Further, there will not be a clear consensus concerning the change goals and change targets, and there is no shared consensus as to how the change is to be produced. Thus, confusion over the use of various techniques to employ will frequently occur.

An immature relationship is also characterized by a lack of role clarity and flexibility. Again, there is no consensus on the part of the change agent and the client system of their assumed roles. There is a lack of clarity on the part of the change agent to assume the role of educator/trainer, model, technical expert. A lack of clarity also exists on the part of the change agent concerning the assumed roles of resource provider, supporter/advocate, and information supplier. Further, a lack of consensus as to the mutual role to be played, such as learner, frequently exists.

An immature change relationship occurs when low role flexibility is encountered. This is often experienced by many practitioners. Situations that occur where clients will not allow change agents to assume more than one role, such as the role of technical expert, will obviously inhibit the change relationship. Lack of flexibility can also occur when the change agent does not allow the client to assume other roles, e.g., not allowing the client the freedom to become a supporter/advocate, learner, or participant. This will almost certainly cause a diminished return on the OD investment.

It is reasonable to assume that full change maturity may not be fully achievable. What is achievable, however, is the commitment and actions taken when striving toward change maturity. Given the dynamic nature of any planned intervention, changes on the part of the organization will change the roles and task of the change agent and client system. As all relationships evolve, so do relationships in organizational change.

Consequences of a Mature Change Relationship

There is, as every organizational development practitioner knows, a broad range of consequences of a mature change relationship. The effectiveness of an organizational intervention is often a function of how well the change agent and client system have played their respective roles. These roles are greatly influenced by the skills, values, abilities, needs, resources, education, and background and experience of all parties. There are six major consequences of the way in which the parties have fulfilled their roles and assumed a mature change relationship. These six consequences are task role clarity versus ambiguity, ethical consonance versus ethical dilemmas, trust versus mistrust, role harmony versus role conflict, flexibility versus inflexibility, change success versus change failure.

Task/Role Clarity Versus Ambiguity. When roles are properly structured and communicated, then tasks and roles will be clear to all parties. On the other hand if roles are improperly structured, or poorly communicated, then task, roles, and most of what else is associated with the change effort will become ill-defined and confusing.

Ethical Consonance Versus Ethical Dilemmas. When roles are properly structured and communicated before the actual intervention, then the many possible value conflicts and ethical dilemmas can be avoided. However, when risk, needs, goals, and agendas of change agents and client systems are not properly dealt with, many ethical breaches are possible. Issues such as client confidentiality and misuse of data, are frequently encountered in an immature relationship.

Trust Versus Mistrust. As a result of differing perceptions of personal role requirements, distortions in perceptions often occur. When this happens, mutual distrust is a logical consequence. Needless to say, when trust is absent the desired behavior change will rarely occur. When roles are well structured and communicated, perceptions will be more accurate and trust can be built and maintained.

Role Harmony Versus Role Conflict. As a result of achieving a clear understanding of the role requirements and expectations of both change agents and client systems role harmony can be achieved. Role harmony is the state of a relationship between the change agent and the client system in which both parties have a clear understanding and assume their respective roles. Further, role harmony is not an enduring state of existence, but rather, it fluctuates as the roles of both change agent and client system change in accordance with the OD effort.

Role conflict often occurs in organizational change as a result of the change parties not fulfilling their mutual roles, such as problem solver, diagnostician, or learner. Role conflict is often the result of issues such as needs, values, goals, skills/abilities, inadequate resources, and politicizing the change effort.

Flexibility Versus Inflexibility. Perhaps the most obvious measure of change agents and client systems is role flexibility. When role clarity and harmony are achieved, and clear perceptions and expectations established, the flexibility required for a mature change effort follows. Without properly structured roles and clear expectations and a mutual commitment to the task, change agents and client systems frequently can become trapped by the inflexibility of personal or organizational position.

Change Success Versus Change Failure. The most important consequences of change maturity is change success versus change failure. Many times the change maturity that is achieved between change parties serves as a microcosm of the entire change effort. Change agents and their respective client systems cannot expect the change goals to be met and the organization to learn and adapt unless the relationship between them possesses the same qualities. Given that most change efforts involve diagnosis of organizational problems, and use of acceptable intervention techniques, the variable in question remains the change relationship. The evidence suggests that most organizational change efforts fail not because of poor problem identification or use of inappropriate techniques rather, it is the human element that is the overall greatest determinant in changing organizations.

SUMMARY

It can be concluded that much success or failure in OD is a direct result of the nature of the relationship between the change agent and the client system. The relationship between the change agent and the client system is greatly influenced by such factors as values, needs, goals, skills/abilities, and available resources. These factors tend to make the relationship unique and dynamic, producing many issues which must be dealt with. Issues such as trust, dependency, termination, appropriateness of the intervention, termination and withholding of services, determination of who the client is, and the depth and the scope of the intervention are major obstacles to effective OD, yet provide opportunities for learning and growth.

Dealing with the many factors influencing the change relationship requires that a mature relationship be built between the change agent and the client system. Change maturity can be seen as being comprised of task clarity and specificity, as well as role clarity and flexibility. Through successful attempts to achieve high change maturity, a number of positive consequences can result. Task clarity, role clarity, ethical consonance, trust, role harmony, flexibility, and overall intervention success can be achieved through conscious and collaborative efforts.

NOTES

Alderfer, C. P. "Organization Development." *Annual Review of Psychology* 28, 1977, 197–223.

Argyris, C. *Intervention Theory and Method.* Reading, Mass.: Addison-Wesley, 1970.

Argyris, C. "Explorations in Consultant/Client Relationship." *Human Organization* 20, no. 31, 1961, 121–33.

Argyris, C. and Schon, P. A. *Organizational Learning: A Theory of Action Perspective.* Reading, Mass.: Addison-Wesley Publishing Co., 1978.

Bales, R. F. *Interaction Process Analysis: A Method for the Study of Small Groups.* Cambridge, Mass.: Addison-Wesley, 1950.

Beckhard, R. *Organization Development: Strategies and Models.* Reading, Mass.: Addison-Wesley, 1969.

Bennis, W. G. *Organization Development: Its Nature, Origins, and Prospects.* Reading, Mass.: Addison-Wesley, 1969.

Blake, R. R. and Mouton, J. S. *The Managerial Grid.* Houston, Tex.: Gulf Publishing Co., 1964.

Blake, R. R. and Mouton, J. S. *Consultation.* Reading, Mass.: Addison-Wesley, 1976.

Bowen, D. D. "Value Dilemmas in Organizational Development." *Journal of Applied Behavioral Science* 13, no. 4, 1977, 543–56.

Bowers, D. G. "OD Techniques and Their Results in 23 Organizations." The Michigan ICC Study. *Journal of Applied Behavioral Science* 9, no. 2, 1973, 21–43.

Bowers, D. G. "Organizational Development: Promises, Performance, Possibilities." *Organizational Dynamics* 4, 1976, 50–63.

Ford, C. H. "Developing a Successful Client-Consultant Relationship." *Human Resource Management* 13, no. 2, 1974, 2–11.

French, W. "Organization Development: Objectives, Assumptions, and Strategies." *California Management Review* 12, 2, 1969, 23–34.

French, W. L. and Bell, C. H. Jr. *Organization Development*. 2d. ed. Englewood Cliffs, N.J.: Prentice-Hall, 1976.

Friedlander, F. and Brown, L. D. Organizational Development. *Annual Review of Psychology* 25, 1974, 315–41.

Gallessich, J. *The Profession and Practice of Consultation*. San Francisco, Cal.: Jossey-Bass Publishers, 1982.

Griener, L. E. "Patterns of Organizational Change." *Harvard Business Review* 45, no. 7, 1967, 119–28.

Harrison, R. "Choosing the Depth of the Organizational Intervention." *Journal of Applied Behavioral Science* 6, no. 2, 1970, 182–202.

Hersey, P. and Blanchard, K. H. *Management of Organization Behavior*. Englewood Cliffs, N.J.: Prentice-Hall, 1976.

Huse, E. F. *Organization Development and Change*. 2d ed. St. Paul: West, 1980.

Kaplan, A. *The Conduct of Inquiry*. San Francisco, Cal.: Chandler Publishing Co., 1964.

Kaplan, R. E. "Stages in Developing a Consulting Relationship: A Case of a Long Beginning." *Journal of Applied Behavioral Science* 14, no. 1, 1978, 43–60.

Korman, A. K. "Consideration, Initiating Structure, and Organizational Criteria—A Review." *Personal Psychology* 27, 1966, 349–361.

Likert, R. *New Patterns of Management*. New York: McGraw Hill, 1961.

Lippitt, G. L. *Organizational Renewal: A Holistic Approach to Organizational Development.* Englewood Cliffs, N.J.: Prentice-Hall, 1982.

Lippitt, G. L. and Lippitt, R. *The Consulting Process in Action.* La Jolla, Cal.: University Associates, 1978.

Margulies, N. and Raia, A. *Organizational Development: Values, Process, and Technology.* New York: McGraw-Hill, 1972.

Margulies, N. and Raia, A. *Conceptual Foundations of Organizational Development.* New York: McGraw-Hill, 1978.

Menzel, R. K. "A Taxonomy of Change Agent Skills." *Journal of European Training* 4, no. 5, 1975, 287-88.

Michael, D. and Mirvis, P. "Changing, Erring, and Learning." In Mirvis and Berg (eds.), *Failures In Organization Development and Change: Cases for Essays for Learning.* New York: John Wiley & Sons, 1977, 311-34.

Mill, C. R. "Feedback: The Art of Giving and Receiving Help." In C. Bell, and L. Nadler, (eds.) *The Client-Consultant Handbook.* Houston, Tex.: Gulf Publishing Company, 1979.

Milstein, M. M. and Smith D. "The Shifting Nature of OD Contracts: A Case Study." *Journal of Applied Behavioral Science* 15, no. 2, 1979, 179-83.

Porras, J. J. "The Impact of Organization Development: Research Findings." *Academy of Management Review* 2, no. 3, 1978, 249-66.

Schein, E. H. *Process Consultation: Its Role In Organization Development.* Reading, Mass.: Addison-Wesley, 1969.

Stogdill, R. and Coons, A. (eds.) *Leadership Behavior: Its Description and Measurement.* Columbus: Bureau of Business Research, Ohio State University, 1957.

Tichy, N. M. "Agents of Planned Social Change: Congruence of Values, Cognitions, and Actions." *Administrative Science Quarterly* 18, no. 2, 1974, 164-82.

Walton, R. F. "Interpersonal Peacemaking." *Confrontations and Third Party Consultation.* Reading, Mass.: Addison-Wesley, 1969.

Warrick, O. D. and Donovan, T. "Surveying OD Skills." *Training and Development Journal* 33, no. 9, 1979, 22-25.

Weisbord, M. "The Organization Development Contract." *Organization Development Practitioner* 5, no. 2, 1973, 1-4.

6

Ethical Dilemmas
in OD Practice

INTRODUCTION

In previous chapters the training and education of OD consultants and their values have been discussed. Values have also been approached from the client system perspective. The synergism of training, values, and the resultant roles assumed by the consultant and client system create for all concerned parties considerable questions of ethicality. The questions of ethics in the OD profession have been dealt with by numerous scholars (Warwick and Kelman, 1973; Walton and Warwick, 1973; Atkins and Kuriloff, 1975; Shay, 1965; Pfeiffer and Jones, 1977; Zaltman and Duncan, 1976; Mosley, 1970; Miles, 1979; Maidment and Losito, 1980; Wooten and White, 1983). However, the reciprocal nature of the roles of consultants and client system will be emphasized here to show the impact of the roles on the ethical questions faced by both parties to the consulting contract.

ETHICAL DILEMMAS

A Working Definition

Unfortunately, the vast majority of literature involved with ethics in organizational development, as well as ethics in general, do not adequately serve the definitional needs to investigate ethics in organizational change. Walton and Warwick (1973) maintain that ethical dilemmas arise from the role of consultant to management while attempting to enhance "humanistic values in the organization." Lippitt and Lippitt (1978) see these dilemmas as being derivatives of disagreements between the change agent and client system concerning expectations of both parties about the consulting process. Mirvis and Seashore (1979), who discuss organizational research, see ethical dilemmas as resultants of involvement in multiple roles, while Warwick and Kelman (1973) maintain that ethical dilemmas result from value conflicts. Lippitt (1982) defines ethics "as a set of standards or codes, or value system by which free, human actions are determined as ultimately right or wrong, good or evil. If an action agrees with these standards, it is an ethical action; if it does not agree, it is an unethical action" (p. 364). Therefore, values influence assumed roles which then impact upon appropriate roles. An ethical dilemma then involves a choice of what is acceptable or unacceptable behavior for the change agent or client system. This may or may not result in an ethical breach, which occurs only when the act on the part of a professional transgresses a law, role, standard, or established norm. This definition then begins to focus upon the integral nature of consultant value system and their impact upon the roles that a consultant feels is appropriate in an intervention effort. Moreover, client systems have a set of values that define for them their role in the intervention and the role that they as a client expect from the consultant. It is no small wonder then that both the consultant and the client system face a multitude of ethical dilemmas, when indeed there are scant guidelines concerning what is appropriate.

Major Categories of Ethical Dilemmas

While many authors have discussed professional ethics in organizational development, more analysis is needed concerning the types of ethical dilemmas that occur. Reviewing the work in organizational development, consulting, and training and development the beginnings of some consistency in thought and form are present. Although ranging considerably in terminology, the dilemmas and unethical practices have focused on certain areas of concern. Generally, five types of ethical dilemmas in organizational development practice have been observed and described by practitioners and scholars. These five categories of ethical dilemmas can be seen to result from role episodes, that occur between change agents and client systems. They are: (1) misrepresentation and collusion, (2) misuse of data, (3) manipulation and coercion, (4) value and goal conflict, and (5) technical ineptness.

Misrepresentation and Collusion

This category of ethical question is a pervasive and widely occurring dilemma in organizational development practice (Shay, 1965; Pfeiffer and Jones, 1977; French and Bell, 1978; Miles, 1979; Maidment and Losito, 1980). It may become manifest in three forms. First, misrepresentation and collusion occurs when the change agent misrepresents his/her skill base. This occurs when the change agent overstates his/her education, experience, certification, or specialized training. Likewise, misrepresentation takes place when the client system misrepresents the organization's interest, goals, or needs.

These "prior to the OD program" occurrences usually take the form of exaggerated intervening claims. For example, Miles (1979) has concluded based upon an analysis of previous work by Bowers (1977) that ". . . interveners may, to gain entry and sell their services, make inflated claims for what OD can accomplish. This amounts to misrepresentation of services to be offered." (p. 441).

Those individuals representing the organization also face critical ethical questions. Initially, a decision must be made to launch an OD program. This decision according to Miles (1979) ". . . is characteristically made by a small group of managers . . . and one or more consultants" (p. 441). This approach inevitably suggests questions concerning whose interest will be served and at what level in the organization. Commenting upon this, Huse (1975) notes:

> Most OD consultants consider the entire social system to be their client system—that they are working for the total organization rather than for the individual manager. Nevertheless, they are paid as management consultants and may find themselves in a real role conflict as to just what the client is. (p. 72)

Misrepresentation and collusion also occurs where the change agent or the client system, attempts to exclude outside parties for personal gain or protection. Collusion may also occur when objectivity is lost. This can occur through assimilation of the change agent into the organizational culture of the client system. This type of inappropriate structuring of the relationship between the change agent and the client system may increase avoidance of unresolved issues and increases the probability of collusion between the change agent and members of the client system. "Moreover, client values may cause a particular structuring of information that presents a biased view about the nature and source of problems" (Zaltman and Duncan, 1976, p. 333).

Misuse of Data

The second major category of ethical dilemmas in organizational change is misuse of data. Shay (1965), Walton and Warwick (1973), Zaltman and Duncan (1976), and Pfeiffer and Jones (1977) have investigated this dilemma as it relates specifically to organizational development. Walton and Warwick have noted that, "Under some conditions . . . the information obtained by OD may be a tool of administration or repression" (p. 686). Misuse of data in organizational development occurs when the voluntary consent or confidentiality of the client system is violated or abridged.

Misuse of data as a breach of ethics in organizational development may also occur for two other reasons. First, it may occur when data collected are distorted, deleted, or not reported by either the client system or the change agent. Second, misuse of data may occur when the data are used to punitively assess persons or groups that render personal, professional, or organizational harm. Data such as personality traits, career interest, and market information are frequent examples. Walton and Warwick (1973) state that "in the typical OD scenario such information is to be collected in an atmosphere of trust, where no one will be harmed by his honesty or by revelations . . . but trust has its limits and administrators are human" (p. 686). Huse (1975) describes such a dilemma:

> My own experience as a consultant has placed me in such moral dilemmas. One involved a situation in which a manager wanted to obtain information about his own managerial style so that he could improve the way in which he worked with his subordinates. The request was prompted by a performance appraisal that he had with his immediate supervisor. Since I had been in the organization only a short time, I was not certain about the trust level of the subordinates. The subordinates and I held a meeting at which I explained the supervisor's

desire to "get a reading" on his style. We also talked about whether or not they really wanted to respond to his request. It was finally decided that they would do so, but that the data gathering would be done by interview rather than by questionnaire, since we had established that they did not yet trust me sufficiently to complete a questionnaire which might identify them through their handwriting or some other source. We also agreed that I would feed back the information to them before giving it to the boss: this would ensure both that no one person could be identified and that the data represented the feelings and perceptions of the group as a whole. This process allowed the group to decide whether or not they wanted to accede to the request and also provided them with assurance that the data would remain confidential. (p. 73)

Manipulation and Coercion

Manipulation and coercion constitute the third major category of ethical dilemmas in organizational development (Walton and Warwick, 1973; Lippitt and Lippitt, 1978; Warwick and Kelman, 1973; Huse, 1975; Zaltman and Duncan, 1976; and Pfeiffer and Jones, 1977). Manipulation and coercion have received more attention than several other dilemmas due to their relatedness to other types of dilemmas as well as their philosophical connotation. Basically, manipulation and coercion occur when the organizational development effort requires organizational members against their will to abridge their personal values or needs resulting in personal, professional, or organizational harm. Forced participation in a change effort such as sensitivity training is exemplary. Closely related are examples in which the OD effort changes the personal attributes or the structure and process in a social system without voluntary participation or consent of organizational members affected. Zaltman and Duncan (1976) maintain that all OD strategies involve manipulation, and that the basic question should be "under what conditions are particular forms of manipulation warranted" (p. 331). Kelman (1965) has also noted that manipulation is always present by stating, "the two horns of the dilemma, then, are represented by the view that any manipulation of human behavior inherently violates a fundamental value, but that there exists no formula for so structuring an effective change situation that such manipulation is totally absent" (p. 33).

Value and Goal Conflict

The fourth major category of ethical dilemmas in organizational development is value and goal conflict (Lippitt and Lippitt, 1978; Benne, 1959; Warwick and Kellman, 1973; Zaltman and Duncan, 1976; and Pfeiffer and Jones, 1977). Lippitt and Lippitt state that

> ... the consultant is a maker of value judgments. Consulting involves activities in which choices must be made between alternative courses of action. When choosing between possible alternatives, a consultant is making a choice between two or more values. (p. 59)

This type of value and goal conflict can occur when there is ambiguity of conflict concerning whose values will be maximized by the change effort, or whose needs will be fulfilled by meeting such goals. Value and goal conflict also occurs when there is conflict or ambiguity in defining change goals or choosing an intervention target. According to Pfeiffer and Jones (1977) "consultants need to determine what the values of a client organization are, and if they cannot accept those values, either they have to get out or they have to try to change the organization's values" (p. 222). Another form of this type of dilemma is when conflict or ambiguity results in the inflexibility to alter change strategies on the part of the change agent or client system, or when the change agent or client system withholds services or needed resources. The change agent, for example, may have his/her ego involved in a particular change strategy in a way that prevents them from changing strategies when evidence suggests an alternate method. Likewise the client system because of self protection or for budgeting reasons might withhold cooperation for resources necessary to the OD effort.

Technical Ineptness

The fifth major type of ethical dilemma in organizational development is technical ineptness. Technical ineptness is the most widely written about type of ethical dilemma (Benne, 1959; Shay, 1965; Mosely, 1970; Walton and Warwick, 1973; Lippitt and Lippitt, 1978; Warwick and Kellman, 1973; Huse, 1973; Zaltman and Duncan, 1976; Pfeiffer and Jones, 1977; French and Bell, 1978; Maidment and Losito, 1980). Technical ineptness may occur when there is a lack of knowledge or skill in the use of techniques and procedures to effectively diagnose social systems problems, formulate change targets, choose and utilize the proper change technology and strategy, or intervene in the social system at the appropriate depth and scope. Zaltman and Duncan (1976) state that "in many ways the diagnosis of the problem determines the general outline of the solution(s) and in this indirect way is related to the outcome" (p. 322).

Technical ineptness may also occur when there is an inability to effectively evaluate an intervention, or terminate an organizational development relationship. This dilemma may also result from an inability to ensure the proper reduction of dependency and to engage in the proper transition and monitoring of the change effort to internal parties. Lippitt (1982) notes that "the success of any human system renewal effort depends to a great extent on the qualifications and performance of the persons doing the initiating and the planning" (p. 173).

A Model for the Study of Ethical Dilemmas

Once a common framework for investigating change has been established, agent/client system behaviors have been developed, the definition of an ethical dilemma described, and the various types of ethical dilemmas delineated, a relevant question is how do they occur? The literature of OD illustrates little consensus concerning the ways in which ethical dilemmas might present themselves. Figure 6.1 is an attempt to illustrate in a causal sequence the occurrence of ethical dilemmas. As shown, Figure 6.1 depicts the antecedents, processes, and the consequences involved in the occurrence of ethical dilemmas.

Antecedents are used in this context as uncommunicated and therefore unresolved differences in values, goals, or needs of the change agent and client system. These antecedent conditions might also exist when the change agent does not fully disclose the limits of his/her skills and abilities or where the client system does not fully disclose the extent of available resources that the client system is willing to devote to the change effort. Processes, on the other hand,

FIG. 6.1. A Role Episodic Model of Ethical Dilemmas in Organizational Development

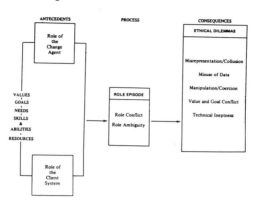

Source: From Wooten, K. C. and White, L. P. "Ethical Problems In The Practice of Organization Development." *Training and Development Journal* 37, no. 4, 1983, p. 19.

is the resultant role episode that occurs between the change agent and client system. Figure 6.1 shows this role episode as role conflict unresolved differences in values, goals, needs, skills and abilities, or undisclosed resource limitations. More specifically, role ambiguity refers to a behavior exchange between the change agent and the client system where there is a lack of sufficient information for one or both role occupants to fulfill the called for role to the fullest.

Role theory, as discussed by Katz and Kahn (1966), has served a variety of purposes. It has been used, for example, to analyze ethical dilemmas occurring in organizational research (Mirvis and Seashore, 1979). The idea can be extended to also illustrate the occurrence of ethical dilemmas as resultants of role episodes. Role theory provides a vehicle to explain the behavioral exchanges between a change agent and client system which may occur in any change effort. These role episodes are part of the client-consultant relationship wherein the change agent and the client system communicate or do not communicate various role expectations for each other, depending on the nature of the change effort and on the nature of their relationship.

As shown in Figure 6.1 the variety of antecedents for ethical dilemmas in organization development moderate the relationship between the change agent and client system as they engage in a continuous cycle of sending, receiving, responding, and sending of new interactions. When these factors are in conflict with one another, and if left unresolved, the consequence is confrontation with one or all of the categories of ethical dilemmas.

As shown in Figure 6.1 the five categories of ethical dilemmas previously discussed tend to be observed by practitioners and scholars. Each may be a consequence of the role conflict or ambiguity between the change agent and the client system. Thus, the consequences of role ambiguity and role conflict may be misrepresentation and collusion, misuse of data, manipulation and coercion, value and goal conflict, and/or technical ineptness.

Using the model shown in Figure 6.1, the process leading up to the occurrence of one or more of the categories of ethical dilemmas can be illustrated. The notion of values and the role they play in the OD process have been an important part of the analytical work into the OD profession (Friedlander, 1978; Miles, 1979; Walton and Warwick, 1973; Bowen, 1977; Alderfer, 1977; Conner, 1977). Consider the value and goal orientations of a change agent who might be oriented in the direction of improving the quality of work life, while the value and goal orientation of the client system might be to increase organizational efficiency. The assumed roles of the change agent and client system comprise the antecedents for the process, which is represented as role episode (Fig. 6.1). The created role episode results in role conflict and role ambiguity ending in a consequence of multiple questions of ethicality represented by any or all of the categories of ethical dilemmas, i.e., misrepresentation/collusion, misuse of data, manipulation/coercion, value and goal conflict, technical ineptness. The specific ethical question(s) that might confront the change agent and the client system are dealt with below.

Inventory of, and discussion of the skills and abilities of the change agent are an important part of the initial stages of an OD effort. If these are not clarified, change agents whose expertise is primarily in human relations may manifest behaviors of that role. Concurrently, the client system mistakenly thinks the change agent has a technical orientation (antecedents). This creates a process wherein the change agent and client system experience results in unmet expectations concerning the role each is expected to play. The coupling of these antecedents and processes tends to create an environment characterized by vagueness and questions surrounding the categories of ethical dilemmas.

WHERE ETHICAL DILEMMAS OCCUR

Occurrence of General Dilemmas

In the investigation of how and why ethical dilemmas occur, as well as the nature of ethical dilemmas themselves, information is needed concerning where in the OD process various ethical dilemmas occur. The examination of this question is essentially assessing the probability that general ethical dilemmas will occur at various stages of OD. Moreover, the probability of the occurrence of specific ethical dilemmas is also of equal importance. Such an analysis and framework provides a necessary tool for change agents and client systems alike. Being cognizant of the likelihood of such dilemmas occurring enables change agents and client systems to structure their activities and relationship accordingly. Clearer understanding of why ethical dilemmas occur, how and where they occur, and what they consist of, is of equal importance to both suppliers and consumers of OD services.

Using the ten stages of the process-relational model of organizational change and the five types or categories of ethical dilemmas that typify OD practice, one can assess the likelihood of occurence of certain ethical dilemmas at the various stages. Table 6.1 provides an assessment of the likelihood of occurrence of the five major categories of ethical dilemmas at the ten stages of the OD process. These hypothetical probabilities are based on the actions that typify both the change agent and the client system at each process stage. Although theoretical in nature, one can begin to illustrate, research, investigate, and control the likelihood of the occurrence of each ethical dilemma.

In addition to illustrating the variations in likelihood of each ethical dilemma occurring in the OD process, Table 6.1 illustrates which process stage is likely to be associated with various types of ethical dilemmas. The result of the process stage-ethical dilemma matrix is a clearer understanding of areas of organizational change that require more conscious effort in maintaining role clarity and reducing role conflict between the change agent and the client system.

A view of Table 6.1 indicates that the ethical dilemma of technical ineptness and value and goal conflict, followed closely by misrepresentation/collusion, appears to have the highest probability of

TABLE 6.1. Propensity for Major Ethical Dilemmas at Various Stages of OD

Stage	Misrepre-sentation and Collusion	Misuse of Data	Manipula-tion and Coercion	Value and Goal Conflict	Technical Ineptness
Initiation	very high	very low	very low	high	low
Clarification	very high	very low	very low	very high	moderate
Specification/ Agreement	very high	very low	very low	very high	high
Diagnosis	moderate	very high	low	high	very high
Goal Setting/ Action Planning	very high	high	very low	very high	very high
System Intervention	high	very high	very high	very high	very high
Evaluation	high	very high	very low	low	very high
Alteration	high	moderate	high	high	high
Continuation/ Maintenance	moderate	very low	high	high	moderate
Termination	very low	very low	very low	moderate	very high

occurring. This may be explained by the fact that technical ineptness on the part of the change agent can occur at any stage of OD. Similarly, value and goal conflict may have a higher probability of occurrence since values underlie the very essence of OD itself. At each stage of OD one is dealing with the investigation, change, and maximization of human and organizational values. Moreover, since the OD process can be seen as stages of role episodes involving role sending and role taking, the opportunity for misrepresentation and collusion may also tend to occur with a high frequency.

The ethical dilemma of misuse of data, followed by manipulation/ coercion tend to at least hypothetically, occur with a lesser degree of frequency. It follows that since the activities of data collection, data feedback, data analysis, and data use occur primarily at the stages of diagnosis, goal setting/action planning, and evaluation, that the overall frequency for misue of data may occur less. Similarly, the frequency of manipulation and coercion of organizational members involved in an OD effort seems linked to those stages where the likelihood of manipulation/coercion would occur. The stages involving direct change activities where the change agent has the greatest influence over the personal values of organizational members, appears to reside in the stages of intervention, alteration, and continuation/maintenance.

The overall picture presented by Table 6.1 indicates that ethical dilemmas have the greatest likelihood of occurrence in the stage of intervention, followed by goal setting/action planning, diagnosis, evaluation, and alteration. However, the overall variance in spread of the hypothetical frequency of specific ethical dilemmas to occur at each stage is not as great as the hypothetical spread of probability of ethical dilemmas among the five general categories of ethical dilemmas.

Although it appears plausible that certain ethical dilemmas occur primarily during certain stages of OD, the fairly small variance in probability for ethical dilemmas to occur across all ten stages suggest that each stage of OD has a relatively high likelihood for ethical dilemmas to occur. As shown, the theoretical distribution of very low, low, moderate, high, and very high probability that ethical dilemmas will occur is suggested by role theory tenets. That is, almost any role relationship, regardless of the nature or kind is subject to role ambiguity and role conflict resulting in questions of ethicality.

Occurrence of Specific Dilemmas

To further analyze the process relational properties of OD and ethical dilemmas, Table 6.2 is an attempt to illustrate more specifically the nature of these ethical dilemmas at each stage. Table 6.2 depicts 31 specific ethical dilemmas that might occur at various stages of OD. The table is intended as a heuristic tool for operational diagnosis of the role relationships between the change agent and the client system. In each of the 31 ethical dilemmas the situation surrounding its occurrence is described. As noted earlier, the responsibility for the occurrence of ethical dilemmas resides both with the change agent and the client system. Here, both parties to the OD process must be

TABLE 6.2. Ethical Dilemmas

Stage	Dilemmas	Stage	Dilemmas
Initiation	Misrepresentation of the consultant's skill base and background Misrepresentation of organizational interest	Systems Intervention	Assimilation into culture Inappropriate depth of intervention Coercion vs. choice, freedom, and consent to participate Environmental manipulation
Clarification	Inappropriate determination of who the client is Avoidance of reality testing Inappropriate determination of value orientation		
Specification/ agreement	Inappropriate structuring of the relationship Inappropriate definition of change problem Collusion to exclude outside parties	Evaluation	Misuse of data Deletion and distortion of data
Diagnosis	Avoidance of problems Misuse of data Distortion and deletion of data Ownership of data Voluntary consent Confidentiality	Alteration	Failure to change and lack of flexibility Adoption of inappropriate strategy
Goal setting/ action planning	Inappropriate choice of intervention goal and targets Inappropriate choice of operative means Inappropriate scope of intervention	Continuation/ maintenance	Inappropriate reduction of dependency Redundancy of effort Withholding of services
		Termination	Inappropriate transition of change effort to internal sources Premature exit Failure to monitor change

Source: Adapted from White, L. P. and Wooten, K. C. "Ethical Dilemmas In Various Stages of Organizational Development." *Academy of Management Review* 8, no. 4, 1983, p. 695.

held accountable for their part in a role episode of stages of change. Thus, an ongoing analysis of role behaviors at each stage of the OD effort is necessary in reducing role ambiguity and conflict, and subsequent ethical dilemmas.

Table 6.2 illustrates the variety of specific forms that the dilemma categories of manipulation/coercion, misuse of data, value and goal conflict, misrepresentation and collusion, and technical ineptness take. While it may be argued that several of the 31 specific dilemmas can occur in more than one stage of OD, the presentation of these dilemmas is intended to be normative; that is, that stages of OD progress sequentially as suggested by the process-relational model. On a descriptive level, however, experienced practitioners of OD know of the sometimes unexpected occurrence of events in planned change. This unexpectedness necessitates OD process flexibility in the form of changing roles and role demands, irrespective of stage.

As shown in Table 6.2, the stage of initiation is frequently impaired by various types of misrepresentation. For example, misrepresentation of the consultant's skillbase and misrepresentation on the background of organizational interest can occur. Normatively, the next stage of the OD process is clarification. At this point in the role relationship, there may be problems determining who the client is and the value orientation of the change agent-client system. The avoidance of reality testing on the part of both the change agent and the client system might be another manifestation of misrepresentation. In specification/agreement, the parameters or structure of the relationship between the change agent and client system begins to form and the general definition of the problem is considered. Conditions are conducive at this stage for the change agent and client system to collude to exclude competition and influence from endogenous and exogenous sources.

The diagnosis stage of the OD process is fraught with a wide variety of ethical dilemmas. The change agent and client system face issues surrounding avoidance of diagnosing known problems. This occurs when the change agent and client system through perceptual defense mechanisms deny their own inability or unwillingness to solve a problem. More often the diagnosis stage presents perhaps the environment or set of conditions most conducive to the occurrence of misuse or distortion and deletion of data. This area has drawn the greatest amount of attention in the literature of unethical practices. A skilled researcher can empirically support even the wildest of notions, and in the case of unskilled researchers, mislead, or neglect the measurement of certain necessary variables. Ownership of the data is as well a frequently occurring dilemma for the parties to the change. This occurs when survey feedback or process observation is not shared with all contributing members. On a similar note voluntary consent of organizational members and confidentiality are frequent problems that have received much attention.

During goal setting/action planning, questions concerning the choice of a change goal, of the intervention target, operative means, and the scope of the intervention are prevalent. During this stage collusion of parties, technical ineptness, and value and goal conflict can create dilemmas resulting in inappropriate choice of change goals, targets, depth, and method due to a lack of skill, objectivity, or differing needs and orientations. Moreover, in systems intervention, assimilation into the organization's culture and the loss of objectivity is a constant threat for the change agent, as is the inappropriate depth of the intervention. Frequently mentioned in the OD literature is the notion of free will and informed consent of participating parties in OD activities. The change agent must be sensitive to the potential for involuntary change or psychological or professional harm to organizational members. Moreover, the use of sociotechnical and structural interventions, presents the possibility of environmental manipulation.

Table 6.2 shows the stage of evaluation as similar to the stage of diagnosis, in that the possibility exists for the misuse, deletion, or distortion of data. Table 6.2 illustrates that the stage of alteration also has two dilemmas. They are failure to change or lack of flexibility, and adoption of an inappropriate new strategy. These dilemmas tend to occur when an evaluation suggests that alteration is necessary for full effectiveness of the intervention.

During the final stages of continuation/maintenance and termination, a variety of ethical dilemmas are present. As the change effort progresses through the continuation/maintenance stage reducing dependency is a difficult issue for most change agents to encounter. It involves reduction of effort and withholding of change agent services from the client system. Of specific ethical interest is the issue of the change agent continuing the intensity of a helping relationship or services. The possibility exists for collusion of parties, manipulation and coercion of organizational participants and value and goal conflicts and misuse of a change agent's technical skills.

Finally, the termination of a change effort and the change agent-client system relationship is ethically difficult for a number of reasons. During termination, there may be value and goal conflicts between the change agent and client system. Technical ineptness on the part of the change agent may result in the transition of change to inadequately prepared or unskilled internal parties. Likewise, the change agent could prematurely exit the organization or fail to monitor change longitudinally. Of specific difficulty is the assessment of organizational capability to carry through the long-term aspects of a change effort, including the necessary processes to diagnose and solve problems. Improper assessment of client system health can lead to premature exit on the part of the change agent. This action involves the broader issue of responsibility to the client. Moreover, failure to monitor change is an issue that has long-term implications for not only the effectiveness of the organization but for the science of OD as well.

SUMMARY

This chapter has reviewed various definitions of an ethical dilemma. An analysis of these definitions reveals the common thread that an ethical dilemma is a choice situation for the change agent or client system. In the general sense, ethical dilemmas are seen to group into five major categories. These major categories are misrepresentation/collusion, misuse of data, manipulation and coercion, value and goal conflict, and technical ineptness. A model for the study of ethical dilemmas was discussed. The model was used to demonstrate the ways in which antecedents and processes combine to produce a consequence or the occurrence of one or more of the major categories of ethical dilemmas. Using a process-relational model the relative probability of occurrence of the major dilemma categories was discussed. It was noted that within these categories there are 31 specific dilemmas. These specific dilemmas were likewise analyzed in relation to where in the OD process they were relatively likely to occur.

NOTES

Alderfer, Clayton P. "Organization Development." *Annual Review of Psychology* 28, 1977, 197–223.

Atkins, S. and Kuriloff, A. H. "Backfeed Principles in 'Ethics' of Organizational Development Comment." *Journal of Applied Behavioral Science* 11, no. 1, 1975, 121-23.

Bowen, Donald D. "Value Dilemmas in Organization Development." *The Journal of Applied Behavioral Science* 13, no. 4, 1977, 543-56.

Conner, Patrick E. "A Critical Inquiry into Some Assumptions and Values Characterizing OD." *Academy of Management Review* 2, no. 4, 1977, 635-44.

Friedlander, F. "OD Reaches Adolescence: An Exploration of Its Underlying Values." *Journal of Applied Behavioral Sciences* 1, no. 1, 1978, 7-21.

Huse, E. *Organizational Development and Change.* St. Paul, Minn.: West Publishing Co., 1975.

Katz, D. and Kahn, R. L. *The Social Psychology of Organizations.* New York: John Wiley and Sons, 1966.

Kelman, Herbert C. "Manipulation of Human Behavior: An Ethical Dilemma for the Social Scientist." *Journal of Social Issues* 21, no. 2, 1965, 31-46.

Lippitt, G. L. *Organizational Renewal*, 2nd ed. Englewood Cliffs, N.J.: Prentice-Hall, 1982, p. 364.

Lippitt, G. L. and Lippitt, R. L. *The Consulting Process in Action.* La Jolla, Cal.: University Associates, 1978, 57-74.

Maidment, R. and Losito, W. *Ethics and the Consultant Trainer.* Selected Paper No. 11. Madison, Wis.: American Society for Training and Development, 1980.

Miles, Matthew B. "Ethical Issues in O.D. Intervention." *OD Practitioner.* October, 1979, 1-10.

Mirvis, P. H. and Seashore, S. E. "Being Ethical in Organizational Research." *American Psychologist* 34, no. 9, 1979, 766-80.

Mosley, D. C. "Professional Ethics and Competence in Management Consulting." *California Management Review* 12, no. 3, 1970, 44-48.

Pfeiffer, J. W. and Jones, J. E. "Ethical Consideration in Consulting." In J. E. Jones and J. W. Pfeiffer (eds.), *The 1977 Annual Handbook for Group Facilitators.* La Jolla, Cal.: Associates University, 1977, 219-25.

Shay, P. W. "Ethics and Professional Practices in Management Consulting." *Advanced Management Journal* 30, no. 1, 1965, 13-20.

Walton, R. E. and Warwick. "OD: The Ethics of Organizational Development." *Journal of Applied Behavioral Science* 9, no. 6, 1973, 681-99.

Warwick, D. P. and Kelman, H. C. "Ethics in Social Intervention." In G. Zaltman (ed.), *Processes and Phenomenon of Social Change.* New York: Wiley Inter-science, 1973, 377-449.

Wooten, K. C. and White L. P. "Ethical Problems in the Practice of Organization Development." *Training and Development Journal*, April, 1983, 16-23.

Zaltman, G. and Duncan, R. "Ethics in Social Change." In G. Zaltman and R. Duncan (eds.), *Strategies for Planned Change.* New York: John Wiley and Sons, 1976, 323-77.

7

Dealing with Ethical
and Professional Issues

INTRODUCTION

The previous chapter focused upon the occurrence of ethical dilemmas as a result of the roles of the change agent and client system interaction. Using the ten stages of the process-relational model of organizational change and the five categories of ethical dilemmas that typify OD practice, an assessment was made concerning the likelihood of occurrence of the dilemma categories at the various stages. Inasmuch as these dilemmas frequently confront OD practitioners, there are two fundamental questions that are addressed in this chapter. First, what are the characteristics of the various ethical codes that have been stated by major OD organizations such as the American Psychological Association (APA), American Society for Training and Development (ASTD), Certified Consultants International (CCI), Organizational Development Institute (ODI), and National Training Labs (NTL). And second, to what extent do these codes attend to the aforementioned categories of ethical dilemmas—technical ineptness, coercion/manipulation, misuse of data, value and goal conflict, and misrepresentation/collusion. The answer to these fundamental questions will begin a process of unification of existing codes into a comprehensive statement of the position of the OD profession on the question of an ethical system.

UTILIZATION OF ETHICAL CODES

Characteristics of Ethical Codes in the OD Profession

The analysis of characteristics of the ethical codes will be done using three basic criteria (Table 7.1). These are (1) existence of a comprehensive code, (2) existence of a formal review process, and (3) existence of a formal sanction system. This type of an approach will shed light upon the degree of development in existing codes.

Comprehensive Code

As a criterion for the analysis of ethical code development, the word comprehensive refers to the extent to which practitioner and client systems can rely upon a unified statement to provide answers to questions of ethicality that confront them in the fulfillment of their professional OD obligations. In this regard, the APA, CCI, ASTD, and ODI do not appear to have satisfied this criterion. The APA however, does address each of the three criteria presented in Table 7.1. Their published documents include the following: Ethical Principles in Conduct of Research with Human Participants (1981); Specialty Guidelines for the Delivery of Services (1981); and Ethical Standards of Psychologists (1981). While the Specialty Guidelines (1981) make reference to the field of organizational development, an OD professional actively engaged in an organizational intervention would be hard pressed to synthesize this information when confronted with questions of ethicality.

ODI appears to have made the greatest strides with regard to a comprehensive code through its committee on values in the profession. The work of Gellerman and his associates, and the center for the Study of Ethics in the Professions at the Illinois Institute of Technology are making significant progress. Gellerman's group in particular has solicited input from OD professionals in the formation of The Organizational Development Code of Ethics (1984). While CCI has a published statement (1978), it lacks both breadth and depth in addressing the major categories of ethical dilemmas. Likewise, published statements by NTL (1969) and ASTD (1985) make no mention of OD in their statements. However, NTL Institute endorses the Ethical Standards of Psychologists of the American Psychological Association and urges its members to guide their conduct accordingly (p. 10).

TABLE 7.1. Characteristics of Various Ethical Codes for the OD Profession

Criteria	American Psychological Association	American Society for Training and Development	NTL	Certified Consultants International	International Registry of OD Professionals
A Comprehensive Code	Y	N	P	Y	Y
Formal Review Process	Y	N	P (through APA)	P	N
Formal Sanctions Body	Y	N	P (through APA)	Y	N

Y = Yes   N = No   P = Partial

Formal Review Process

This criterion (Table 7.1) is used here as a description of the process utilized by an OD organization in the event that an alleged breach of the stated ethical code or parts thereof has occurred. More specifically, is there an outlined procedure for the investigation of such incidents? In the case of APA, such a procedure is in place albeit without reference to OD specifically. Likewise, NTL through its link with APA has a review process; however, NTL does not explicitly outline its own procedures. CCI is shown in Table 7.1 as having partially fulfilled this criterion on the basis of the statement "The chairperson of the Committee on Ethics and Discipline is responsible for the execution of this policy" (p. 2). Table 7.1 indicates that ODI does not have a formal review process. In their Code of Ethics it is stated, "The profession does not yet have the monitoring and enforcement structure with sanctions and supports, that such a code would require" (p. 24). However, the organization does recognize the need for such a mechanism.

Formal Sanction System

A corollary to the criterion of a formal sanction system (Table 7.1) is whether or not a particular OD organization has assembled a formal sanctioning body. APA, NTL, and CCI have established the organizational mechanism for a formal sanctioning system to operate. ODI, as noted above, does not have such a mechanism in place. They take the position that there are so many professional associations involved in OD, that a universal sanction system is not likely in the near future. Perhaps the time has arrived for definitive steps in that direction.

Coverage of Major Ethical Categories by Various Codes

The analysis of comprehensiveness of the six selected OD organization ethics statements is shown in Table 7.2. The five major categories of ethical dilemmas of technical ineptness, coercion/manipulation, misuse of data, value and goal conflict, and misrepresentation/collusion are rated on a scale of very thorough coverage, minimal coverage, and no coverage. This type of approach provides a means

TABLE 7.2. Coverage of Major Ethical Dilemma Categories by Various Ethical Codes

Professional Organization	Technical Ineptness	Coercion Manipulation	Misuse of Data	Value and Goal Conflict	Misrepresentation/ Cohesion
American Psychological Association	★	★	★	+	★
American Society for Training and Development	+	−	−	−	+
National Training Labs	★	−	−	−	+
Certified Consultants International	★	★	+	+	+
International Registry of Organizational Development Professionals	★	★	★	★	★

★ Very Thorough   + Minimal Coverage   − Not Covered

to look at potential weaknesses in existing codes, and areas of consideration for change. It should be noted at the outset that ASTD, NTL, and APA do not make reference to the OD profession.

Technical Ineptness

ODI in their Code of Ethics sets the tone for the OD organizations sampled in this analysis. They state to "Recognize the limits of their own competence in providing services and using techniques; neither seek nor accept assignments outside those limits; refer client to other professionals when appropriate" (p. 18). CCI in their policy on Ethics, state "Members shall neither promise nor imply services in areas in which they are not competent" (p. 1). Similarly, the ASTD code of Ethics states, "I will keep abreast of pertinent, new knowledge in the field of Human Resource Development" (p. 398). They further elaborate by taking the position that a member ". . . will accurately represent human resource development activities to individuals, organizations, and/or employers" (p. 398). They further state that members "will keep abreast of pertinent, new knowledge in the field of human resource development." (p. 398). However, no reference to the OD professional is made. The APA in "Standards for Providers of Psychological Services" state that "psychologists shall maintain current knowledge of scientific and professional developments that are directly related to the services they render" (p. 5). Likewise, NTL appears to have established a specific stance on the ethical dilemma category of technical competence. Again the codes would be acceptable if the OD profession was included.

In total, as summarized in Table 7.2, most of the codes established by the OD organizations being sampled place great emphasis upon technical competence, albeit without reference to OD as noted.

Coercion/Manipulation

This dilemma presents itself in the form of a decision concerning the exercise of the "free will" of organizational members. With respect to this ethical dilemma category, APA offers the most explicit position statement. By their code a psychologist must be sensitive to conflicts of interest, inform consumers of the purpose and nature of a procedure, and acknowledge the freedom of choice of the client. Similarly ASTD, CCI, and ODI have explicit statements concerning this ethical dilemma category. ODI (1984) for example states in their Code of Ethics "fully inform participants in any activity or procedure as to its nature and purpose and freely acknowledge that participants have free choice as to their participation in any activity initiated by an OD professional; acknowledge that choice may be limited with activity initiated by recognized authorities" (p. 20). NTL, on the other hand, in their list of principles from the Ethical Standards of Psychologists of the APA does not include an explicit statement on this ethical dilemma category.

Misuse of Data

The third major category of ethical dilemmas shown in Table 7.2 is misuse of data. This dilemma, or choice situation, requires the change agent or client system to decide what information is used and how it is used. The APA in its Standards for Providers of Psychological Services (1981) state that "providers of psychological services shall establish a system to protect confidentiality of their records" (p. 9). Similarly, ODI (1984) has formulated explicit statements concerning confidentiality and accountability, evaluation, and assessment. CCI (1978) also has a statement concerning this ethical dilemma category, however the position statement is not as comprehensive as APA and ODI. CCI for example states that "members shall protect the originators of confidential materials" (p. 1). NTL, in its list of principles, does not include an explicit statement concerning the misuse of data. ASTD (1985) does not address the issue.

Value and Goal Conflict

This category of ethical dilemmas refers to situations involving a decision concerning the appropriate mix of change agent and client system values and goals as they relate to the overall change effort. ODI (1984) makes a most explicit statement concerning this dilemma category, by acknowledging the importance of ethics and values, by respecting the multiplicity of values within societies, and by acknowledging that differences in professionally relevant values might result in termination of the consulting relationship. APA (1982) states that "I/O [Industrial/Organizational] psychologists, insofar as possible, anticipate possible conflicts of interest and clarify with both users how such conflicts might be resolved" (p. 30). This statement does not address the issue as explicitly as perhaps is needed. ASTD in their code has not addressed the issue, while CCI has minimal coverage. The latter states "client needs shall be primary in designing programs or interventions and shall be periodically reassessed" (p. 1).

Misrepresentation/Collusion

For purposes of this analysis, misrepresentation and collusion presents itself as a choice situation requiring the change agent or client system to decide between options of fully representing all available information and including or excluding various parties involved in the change effort. APA (1982) has two explicit statements governing this ethical dilemma category. First, Industrial/Organizational psychologists must state what can be reasonably expected from the service; second, Industrial/Organizational psychologists when contracting another psychologist must provide a clear statement of the role of the contractor. In the statement on professional unity, CCI (1982) includes the use of other professionals as third parties. In addressing the collusion issue, CCI recommends that the consultant aid in conflict resolution by not taking sides. Further, members of ODI are bound to reveal "goals, costs, risks, limitations, and anticipated outcomes" (p. 20), with the client system. CCI members are similarly bound, albeit less comprehensively. They state "members shall neither promise nor imply services in areas in which they are not competent . . " and members shall engage in practices ensuring rights of all members of a client system rather than supporting some at the expense of others" (p. 1). ASTD states in its code that members ". . . shall accurately represent human resource development activities to individuals, organizations, and/or employers." (p. 398). ASTD (1985) covers misrepresentation and collusion for only elected officers of their organization.

Table 7.2 presents a summary of the coverage by the sample OD organizations relative to the five ethical dilemma categories. Technical ineptness has received thorough coverage in all of the codes that were sampled. Coercion/manipulation is thoroughly covered in three of five codes. Misuse of data is thoroughly covered in two sample OD organizational codes, and minimally covered in one. Value and goal conflict is an area that has received thorough coverage in one code, minimal coverage in two and no coverage in the remaining two codes looked at in this analysis. Misrepresentation and collusion is thoroughly covered in two of the five codes sampled and minimally covered in the remaining three.

The analysis reveals then that progress is being made by various organizations to formulate a code of ethics for OD. A major stumbling block is a lack of collaboration between organizations in this effort. Later, a proposal is discussed to overcome this difficulty through a national OD organization. However, this kind of an approach is not expected in the near future, nor could a code of ethics address all the day-to-day issues that arise during an intervention. A complement to a comprehensive code and an approach that will provide interim relief is to develop strategies for achieving the optimum change agent client system relationship.

INDIVIDUAL APPROACHES TO PRACTICE

Strategies to Achieve Change Maturity

As change agents and client systems progress from one stage of change to another, and as professional and ethical issues arise, codes of conduct themselves will not totally assist the change parties in on-the-spot decisions that have implications for the effectiveness of the intervention. Since codes of conduct can only guide behavior, and act as a referent for it, specific strategies must be employed by change agents and client systems to ensure proper dealing with professional and ethical issues, via change maturity. As noted in Chapter 5, change maturity is defined as an attempt to achieve a high degree of task clarity/specificity and role clarity/flexibility.

How then is change maturity achieved? To answer this question, change agents and client systems must engage in two actions. First, they must strive to constantly diagnose their relationship and its effectiveness relative to the overall change effort. Second, change agents and client systems must employ specific strategies to enhance their relationship and subsequent level of change maturity. Achieving change maturity cannot be reached as a final state, but rather is a process which requires all parties to continuously diagnose their relationship and utilize needed strategies to strengthen that relationship.

To diagnose the change relationship, change agents and client systems must ask themselves five crucial questions. They are: (1)

where are we in the change relationship; (2) how well are we working together; (3) what effect does each party's needs, values, goals, skills/abilities, and resources have on the relationship; (4) what issues are inhibiting the change relationship; and (5) what does each party need to do in order to enhance the change relationship. Only by consciously addressing these questions can change maturity be achieved.

The first question, of where the change agent and the client system are in the change relationship is of major significance. The change agent and client system must be aware of the development of their relationship in relation to the total change effort. When intervention into the organization has already begun, and the relationship between the change agent and client system have not yet been established, less than optimal change outcomes can be expected.

The second major question used to diagnose the relationship relates most directly to their respective roles. Attention should be given to how well each party is playing its role. It is important that the change agent play the role of technical expert and diagnostician in a manner that will sufficiently address organizational needs. Further, the client system must provide the resources, and be fully engaged in the role of participant to the extent necessary. Are both parties fully portraying their mutual roles of monitor, learner, etc? Finally, change agents and client systems must investigate whether their roles are clear and specific, and whether there is sufficient task clarity and specificity.

The third question to diagnose the relationship involves the factors which influence the relationship itself. The values, goals, needs, skills/abilities, and resources of both parties should be explored at each major stage of the diagnosis, intervention and evaluation. Effort should be made to explore how the values of the change agent and values of the client system are inhibiting or enhancing the relationship itself. Additionally, the extent to which there is conflict between goals, values, and needs as well as deficiencies in skill/abilities or resources should be fully investigated by the change party.

The fourth question to be asked in the diagnosis of the change relationship is perhaps the most difficult and threatening for the change agent and the client system to explore. Issues such as the trust level between the parties, the terms of the contract, appropriateness and depth of the intervention, and dependency, are sometimes not discussed, since discussion of such issues is perceived as threatening not only the change relationship, but the overall change effort as well. Many change efforts have undoubtedly concluded without some of these major issues being resolved. However, the real need for the change agent and client system is to diagnose which issues, if any, threaten the effectiveness of reaching the change goals. Without resolution of these issues, both the relationship and the overall change effort will suffer.

The fifth question to be asked in the diagnosis of the change relationship is a prescriptive one. Exploring what each party needs to do in order to enhance the relationship is often quite helpful. Answers to these questions might range from engaging in different roles to clarifying tasks and responsibilities. More importantly, the question might involve what each party in the relationship is capable of doing. For example, if more resources (information, money, time, etc.) are required, yet are not available, the alternatives and options must be explored by the change parties in order to enhance the relationship.

The answers to these five key questions provide a means by which shared conceptualization involving high task clarity/specificity and high role clarity/flexibility might be obtained. A variety of strategies can be employed by the change agent and the client system in working towards change maturity. Figure 7.1 illustrates these various strategies.

As shown, there are four strategies that can be employed by change agents and client systems in working towards an increasingly mature relationship. These strategies are confronting, reviewing/revising, clarifying/specifying, and resolving. Each of these strategies might be used independently or in combination with one another.

FIG. 7.1. Strategies to Achieve Change Agent Client System Maturity

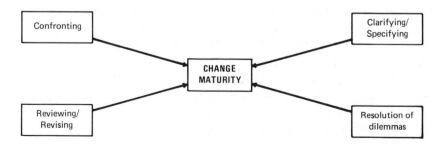

Interestingly, the use of these strategies requires some degree of interpersonal skill to initiate and employ. Moreover, each requires some degree of risk on the part of both the change agent and the client system.

Confronting

The strategy of confronting requires that either the change agent or the client system bring to the other party's level of awareness a problem with the change effort or with the change relationship. Change agents or client systems should, in order to develop the change relationship, use the confrontation meeting. According to Walton (1969) "confrontation refers to the process in which parties directly engage each other and focus on the conflict between them" (p. 95). A confrontation meeting can be utilized in the change relationship to clarify and explore conflicting issues and the types of feelings generated by the conflict itself.

Applied directly to the relationship between the change agent and the client system, confrontation represents a risky, yet sometimes essential synergy required for needed change to occur. Confrontation may in fact lead to termination of the relationship itself. However, confrontation between change parties should involve discussion of the money factors influencing the relationship (e.g., needs, goals, etc.), and the many issues that will occur (e.g., dependency, trust, etc.). Confrontation, due to its risky nature, should be used only when the strategies of clarifying/specifying and reviewing/revising have not produced the desired change. Confrontation is also appropriate when there is a limited amount of time to employ another strategy, and when reluctance to act would prove harmful to the client or to the change relationship.

Essential to utilizing the strategy of confrontation is the effective use of feedback. Effective feedback to the client system or change agent concerning issues or influencing factors gives the other party information about some aspect of their behavior and its impact on the relationship (Mill, 1979). There are a number of criteria to follow in providing effective feedback. Among these is the use of descriptive versus evaluative data, specific information rather than general content, information concerning behavior the other party can control, timeliness of the information, and feedback to see if information is clearly sent and received.

There are in addition to the effective use of feedback several key ingredients to utilizing confrontation in the change relationship. A difficult decision must frequently be made as to whether or not confrontation will cause more resistance or lack of change than avoidance of the issues. When a decision is made that confrontation is appropriate, there are a variety of underlying psychological mechanisms involved. Walton (1969) notes that there are seven ingredients that are strategies to a productive confrontation. They are: (1) mutual positive motivation; (2) balance in situational power of the two principals; (3) synchronization of the confrontation efforts; (4) appropriateness of the differentiation and integration phase of dialogue; (5) conducting openness in dialogue; (6) reliable communication signs; and (7) optimum tension in the situation.

How then would a change agent or client system employ this traditional OD technique to the change relationship? Although there could potentially be many ways of employing confrontation, it is suggested that procedures such as those suggested by Beckhard (1967) be followed. Beckhard suggests the use of a six step procedure be applied to the change relationship. They are: (1) a climate-setting session; (2) information collection; (3) information sharing; (4) priority setting and action planning; (5) immediate follow-ups; and (6) a progress review.

Reviewing/Revising

Reviewing/revising should be a frequently used strategy to achieve change maturity throughout any intervention. At each major stage or phase of the change effort, regularly scheduled reviews should be utilized. This strategy accomplishes two major goals of the OD process. First, the reviewing of past behavior in the relationship and its effectiveness gives both the change agent and the client system a clear idea of past errors, and a clearer vision for increased effectiveness for the future. Second, it provides for feedback to both the change parties. A structured time and place for feedback is important to reach the learning goals in most efforts. Unfortunately, feedback is all too frequently given only in the later stages of an intervention and opportunities to act on relevant learning experiences are missed.

Noting the level of feedback as a result of inadequate review of the change relationship, Argyris (1972) maintains that great anxiety in the relationship is often produced. He posits that an effective intervention strategy makes use of frequent feedback and review of progress. He states that "interventionists tend to fear being kept in the dark by their clients, especially in regard to their effectiveness or ineffectiveness. In the case of the former, if they are not told, they never know why their relationship is not going well and they can do little to correct the relationship" (p. 134).

Only through review of the change progress and the change relationship can revisions be made in either. All too frequently neither the change agent nor the client system know until it's too late that alternative actions and behaviors could have made a significant difference in accomplishing the OD goals. Employing this strategy on a continuing basis is, as noted by Micheal and Mirvis (1977), complementary to the energizing model of OD. Further, employment of frequent reviewing/revising strategies relates directly to the exploration of "personal theories of action" as developed by Argyris and Shon (1978). In essence, employing this strategy means that change agents and client systems will move into more collaborative change modes, and subsequently greater change maturity.

Clarifying/Specifying

Very closely related to the strategy of reviewing/revising is the strategy of clarifying/specifying. This strategy requires both the change agent and the client system to remain constantly aware of their role and their tools. This strategy makes use of role analysis and task analysis on a frequent basis, due to the inordinate amount of change in roles and tasks that will occur. Periodic attempts to clarify what roles are to be played, and how they are to be played are essential. Equally important for the change agent and client system is the determination of under what conditions and for what time frame should role and task analysis be used.

Regularly scheduled interchanges between the change parties must also involve exploration into the task itself. Inevitably, success or failure with the task will affect the relationship itself. Attempts to clarify and specify where the intervention is in terms of progress towards goals is paramount. Further, specifying the depth and the scope of intervention techniques and methods as a collaborative exchange is strongly advised. Attempts to clarify and specify such topics as identifying the target groups at various stages of change, and what are the organizational variables that are of most concern will provide a fruitful exchange.

Resolution of Dilemmas

The fourth strategy to achieve change agent-client system maturity is resolution of dilemmas. This strategy is similar to the strategy of confronting in that it should be used selectively, whereas reviewing/revising and clarifying/specifying should be an on-going strategy. Dilemmas to be resolved are many in nature. Dilemmas, whether of an ethical nature or not, can result from the factors influencing the change relationship (values, goals, etc.) or issues in the change relationship (trust, dependency, etc.). However, resolution of dilemmas frequently offer an opportunity to achieve a richer, more mature relationship. As noted by Argyris (1970) "one possibility that the interventionist may consider is to turn a dilemma into a virtue and to use the dilemma as leverage for the initial interactions between himself and his client" (p. 135).

How then are dilemmas resolved? The answer to this question rests in part with the type of dilemma to be resolved. Since standards of practice and ethical guidelines are not entirely agreed upon, the method of resolution is in most cases left to the change party. Dilemmas may be resolved by two means, however. First, resolutions may be realized by employing past practices. Second, resolution of dilemmas might be found through a negotiated agreement between the change parties. However resolved, the essential aspect of this strategy is that they are resolved as they occur. Unless dilemmas are in fact resolved as they occur, then the vitality and the effectiveness of the change effort will always be in jeopardy.

A Holistic Approach to Professional Practice

With ethical codes to help guide behavior of change agents, strategies to assist in developing change maturity, a holistic approach to professional practice can be suggested. Such an approach utilizes a model for effective OD, as well as a scheme for professional practice. Taken together, a change agent can conceptually and behaviorally guide his/her actions, and the actions of the client system to goal achievement in an organizational intervention.

Figure 7.2 depicts a three dimensional model for effective OD. Shown are three dimensions or kinds of variables which significantly

FIG. 7.2. The Three Dimensional Model for Effective OD

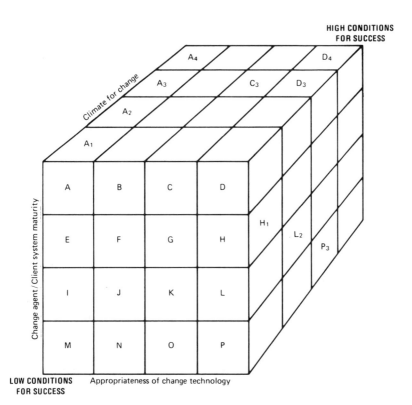

moderate the change effort. Figure 7.2, a three dimensional cube, has within it eighty different cells. Each cell represents a different combination of the three variables shown. These variables are climate for change, change agent-client system maturity, and appropriateness of the change technology. Although many other variables that influence the change process could be added, these three play the predominate role in OD effectiveness.

Of the three major success factors, change agent-client system maturity has been discussed in Chapter 5, with discussion of strategies to build a mature relationship dealt with in the present chapter.

Climate for change refers to both internal and external pressures which produce the need for organizational change programs. Examples of internal pressures may include poor production, labor unrest, employee dissatisfaction, skill deficiencies, poor leadership, poor communication, improper structure or technology, etc. External pressures may include loss of market share, a poor public image, governmental intervention, lack of resources, etc. Internal and external pressures taken together produce a climate, or a readiness to change among the organization's participants. Appropriateness of technology refers to the proper choice of OD techniques for a given problem, target, or goal. Appropriateness of technology also includes choosing the right level and depth of intervention.

What then is known about a change agent's ability to diagnose an organization's climate for change, as well as select the most appropriate change technology? To answer this question, one must investigate the available research on diagnostic measures, as well as the comparative effectiveness of various OD techniques. Although some research exists on the properties of successful and unsuccessful OD, most studies have not dealt with the crucial variables simultaneously. However, a solid argument can be made that unless each of the three crucial success variables are understood and properly dealt with, the success of an intervention is questionable at best.

A review of OD technologies by Beer (1976), and general reviews of OD and its technologies by Friedlander and Brown (1974) and by Alderfer (1976) fully illustrate that as many OD interventions have been unsuccessful as have been successful, irrespective of technologies used. Many of the reasons for not achieving success, have for the most part been attributed to extraneous variables of all types, with much less attention given to the relative absence or presence of the three crucial change variables. There is, however, ample evidence to suggest that successful OD does conceptualize and operationalize each of the three change variables. Griener's (1967) classic study of 18 successful OD interventions well illustrates the necessity for an appropriate change climate vis-à-vis his notion concerning stimulus on the power structure, and the subsequent reaction. This notion is also supported by the work of Franklin (1976). Reviews of OD success (Porros and Berg, 1978; and Golembiewski, Proehl, and Sinil, 1982) as well as studies investigating the differential effects of various OD techniques (Bowers, 1973; and Margulies, Wright, and Scholl, 1977) leaves no question that certain types of OD technologies are more appropriate for certain categories of change variables (i.e., task, structure, people, etc.).

The coding system associated with Figure 7.2 distinguishes each combination of change variables. On the front of the cube, various alphabetic letters illustrate change technology and change maturity combinations. Numbers along the third dimension represent various units of change climate. As such they reference each of the 80 cells depicted by the cube itself. The lower left hand portion of the cube represents the lowest probability for effective change. Therefore, cells at this point of the cube represent the lowest appropriateness of change technology, the lowest level of change maturity, and the poorest climate for change. Conversely, the upper right-hand corner depicts the highest conditions for success. Thus, cell D-4 illustrates an excellent climate for change, a high degree of change maturity, and a high degree of appropriateness of the intervention technology.

Similar to Blake and Mouton's (1976) consulcube, the three dimensional cube can be used as an overall diagnostic device by both change agents and client systems with respect to their intervention effectiveness. As any experienced change agent will attest to, there are numerous accounts of interventions where one of the three crucial "success" variables was lacking. For example, an organization's climate for change might be better than average, the change technology's appropriateness also above average, yet the change agent-client system maturity level at a minimum. On the three dimensional cube, this condition would therefore roughtly approximate cell O-3.

A holistic approach to professional practice necessitates continued awareness by both the change agent and the client system concerning where they are on the OD cube. At various points in the intervention, the change maturity, the climate for change, and even the appropriateness of the change technology may significantly moderate. When such change occurs the potential for professional and ethical dilemmas is heightened. Thus, as an interventions status is diagnosed by use of the three dimensional cube, and strategies employed to deal with ethical dilemmas and professional issues, greater control over the progression of the change effort is possible.

Given the three dimensional model for achieving successful OD, how can practitioners approach a holistic method for achieving success? Table 7.3 depicts a scheme for professional practice in the general sense. This scheme incorporates general activities while Table 7.4 focuses on specific activities involved in professional practice. When

TABLE 7.3. A Scheme For Professional Practice General Activity

Strategies	Dilemmas	Client System Roles	Change Agent Roles	Mutual Roles	Issues	Factors	Diagnostic Variables
Confronting	Misrepresentation/ Collusion	Resource Provider	Educator/ Trainer	Problem Solver	Trust	Values	Climate for Change
Clarifying/ Specifying	Misuse of Data	Supporter Advocate	Model	Diagnostician	Dependency	Goals	Change Maturity
Reviewing/ Revising	Manipulation/ Coercion	Information Supplier	Researcher/ Theoretician	Learner	Termination/ withholding services	Needs	Appropriateness of Change Technology
Resolution of Dilemmas	Value and Goal Conflict	Participant	Technical Expert	Monitor	Contract	Skills and Abilities	
	Technical Ineptness		Resource Linker		Determination of Client	Resources	
					Appreciation of Intervention Means		
					Depth and Level of Intervention		

TABLE 7.4. A Scheme for Professional Practice Specific Activity

Stage	Purpose	Role of Change Agent	Role of Client System	Dilemmas
Initiation	First information sharing	To provide information on background, expertise, and experience	To provide information on possible needs, relevant problems, interest of management and representative groups	Misrepresentation of the consultant's skill base and background Misrepresentation of organizational interest
Clarification	Further elaboration of initiation stage	To provide details of education, licensure, operative values, optimum working conditions	To provide a detailed history of special problems, personnel, marketplace, internal culture, and organizational politics	Inappropriate determination of who the client is Avoidance of reality testing Inappropriate determination of value orientation
Specification/agreement	Sufficient elaboration of needs, interest, fees, services, working conditions, arrangements	To specify actual services, fees to be charged, time frame, actual work conditions	To specify whose needs are to be addressed, goals, objectives, and possible evaluative criteria or end-state outcomes	Inappropriate structuring of the relationship Inappropriate definition of change problem Collusion to exclude outside parties
Diagnosis	To obtain an unfiltered and undistorted view of the organization's problems and processes pinpointing change targets and criterion	To collect data concerning organizational problems and processes, and to provide feedback	To assist change agent in data collection	Avoidance of problems Misuse of data Distortion and deletion of data Ownership of data Voluntary consent Confidentiality
Goal setting/action planning	To establish the specific goals and strategies to be used	To agree mutually with the client system on the goals and strategies to be used	To agree mutually with the change agent on the goals and strategies to be used	Inappropriate choice of intervention goal and targets Inappropriate choice of operative means Inappropriate scope of intervention
Systems intervention	The intervention into ongoing behaviors, structures, and processes	To intervene at specific targets, at a specific depth	To invest the energy and resources required by planned intervention	Assimilation into culture Inappropriate depth of intervention Coercion vs. choice, freedom, and consent to participate Environmental manipulation
Evaluation	To determine the effectiveness of the intervention strategies, energy, and resources used, as well as the change agent-client system relationship	To gather data on specified targets and report findings to the client system	To analyze the evaluation data and determine effectiveness of the intervention	Misuse of data Deletion and distortion of data
Alteration	To modify change strategies, depth, level, goals, targets, or resources utilized if necessary	To make alteration to meet original goals, or to develop new mutual goals and strategies with client system	To make known needs and expectations, and to provide the context for a modification of the original agreement, if necessary	Failure to change and lack of flexibility Adoption of inappropriate strategy
Continuation/maintenance	To monitor and maintain ongoing strategies, provide periodic checks, and continue intervention based on original or altered plans and strategies	To specify the parameters of the continuation of the maintenance of the relationship	To provide or allocate the resources required to maintain or continue the intervention	Inappropriate reduction of dependency Redundancy of effort Withholding of services
Termination	To have the change agent disenfranchise self from the client system and establish a long term monitoring system	To fulfill the role agreed on in previous stages and evaluate overall effectiveness from feedback from the client system	To determine the organization's state of health, and whether it has developed the adaptive change process	Inappropriate transition of change effort to internal sources Premature exit Failure to monitor change

Source: Adapted from White, L. P. and Wooten, K. C. "Ethical Dilemmas in Various Stages of Organizational Development." *Academy of Management Review* 8, no. 4, 1983, p. 695.

184

viewed jointly they illustrate a holistic approach to OD practice in that they provide the context for change agents to view their task, all the variables influencing the task, and how to generally operationalize their task.

Tables 7.3 and 7.4 provide for the change agent and the client system the "big-picture" concerning most of what occurs in an intervention, with prescriptive behaviors noted. Included in the area of general activities are the categories of the three basic diagnostic variables, the four basic strategies to assist change maturity, and the five basic dilemmas which face change agents and client systems that evolve into ethical problems to be resolved. Also, under the categories of general activity, are the respective roles to be played by client systems and change agents, as well as the roles that are to be mutually adopted. Further, Table 7.3 illustrates the seven major issues which continually threaten the change relationship, as well as the five basic factors which influence all change agent-client system roles, actions, and behaviors.

Shown in Table 7.4 are the more distinct behaviors that should occur, and the ethical dilemmas that are most likley to occur. As shown, the ten stages of change are directly correlated with the purpose of each step, and the specific roles of the change agent and client system. Further, the 31 specific ethical dilemmas, as discussed in Chapter 6, are associated with each stage of change. Taken together, Tables 7.3 and 7.4 depict the prescriptive roles, actions, possible dilemmas, and strategies for their resolution.

SUMMARY

In this chapter ethical codes of NTL, CCI, ODI, ASTD, and APA were reviewed in terms of the extent of their coverage of the five major categories of ethical dilemmas. These codes were evaluated using the following criteria: (1) degree of comprehensiveness of the code, (2) presence of a formal review process, and (3) presence of a formal sanction system. The general conclusion reached by the analysis was that all the existing codes are lacking at least in part with regard to their coverage of the major categories of dilemmas. A corollary conclusion reached by the analysis is that a major impetus to ethical behavior of change agents and client systems rests at least in part to the achievement of a mature change relationship, whereupon a model for obtaining this objective was discussed. A schema was presented for how practitioners might approach a holistic method for achieving OD success.

NOTES

Alderfer, C. P. "Change Processes in Organizations." In M. D. Dunnette (ed.), *Handbook of Industrial and Organizational Psychology*. Chicago: Rand McNally, 1976, 1591-1638.

American Psychological Association. *Ethical Principles in the Conduct of Research with Human Participants*. Washington, D.C., 1981.

American Psychological Association. *Ethical Standards of Psychologists*. Washington, D.C., 1981.

American Psychological Association. *Standards for Providers of Psychological Services*. Washington, D.C., 1981.

American Psychological Association, Committee on Professional Standards. *Specialty Guidelines for the Delivery of Services*. Washington, D.C., 1981.

American Society for Training and Development. *Code of Ethics. 1985 Who's Who in Training and Development*. Alexandria, Va.: 1985, p. 398.

Argyris, C. *Intervention Theory and Method: A Behavioral Science View*. Reading, Mass.: Addison-Wesley, 1970.

Argyris, C. and Schon, D. A. *Organizational Learning: A Theory of Action Perspective*. Reading, Mass.: Addison-Wesley, 1978.

Beckard, R. "Confrontation Meeting." *Harvard Business Review* 45, no. 2, 1967, 149-55.

Beer, M. "The Technology of Organizational Development." In M. D. Dunnette (eds.), *Handbook of Industrial and Organizational Psychology*. Chicago: Rand McNally, 1976, 937-94.

Blake, R. P. and Mouton, J. S. *Consultation*. Reading, Mass.: Addison-Wesley, 1976.

Bowers, D. G. "O.D. Techniques and Their Results in 23 Organizations: The Michigan ECL Study." *Journal of Applied Behavioral Science* 9, no. 2, 1973, 21-43.

Certified Consultants International. *Policy on Ethics, Policy Manual.* Stanford, Conn.: March, 1978, pp. 1-2.

Franklin, J. L. "Characteristics of Successful and Unsuccessful Organization Development." *Journal of Applied Behavioral Science* 12, no. 4, 1976, 471-92.

Friedlander, F. and Brown, L. D. "Organizational Development." *Annual Review of Psychology* 25, 1974, 313-41.

Golembiewski, R. T. and Proehl, G. W., Jr. and Sinil, D. "Estimating the Success of OD Applications." *Training and Development Journal* 36, no. 4, 1983, 86-95.

Griener, L. E. "Patterns of Organization Change." *Harvard Business Review* 45, no. 3, 1967, 119-28.

Margulies, N., Wright, P. L., and Scholl, R. W. "Organization Development Techniques: Their Impact on Change." *Group and Organization Studies* 2, 1977, 449-70.

Michael, D. and Mirvis, D. "Changing, Earning and Learning." In Philip H. Mirvis and David M. Berg (eds.), *Failure in Organization Development and Change.* New York: John Wiley, 1977.

Mill, C. R. "Feedback: The Art of Giving and Receiving Help." In C. R. Bell, and L. Nadler (eds), *The Client/Consultant Handbook.* Houston, Tex.: Gulf Publishing Co., 1979.

The International Registry of Organization Development Professionals and Organization Development Handbook. *The Organizational Development Code of Ethics.* Cleveland, Ohio, 1984, pp. 15-26.

National Training Laboratory. *Standards for the Use of Laboratory Method.* Washington, D.C., October 1969, p. 14-15.

Porras, J. I. and Berg, P. O. "Evaluation Methodology in Organizational Development: An Analysis and Critique." *Journal of Applied Behavioral Science* 14, no. 2, 1978, 151-73.

Walton, R. E. *International Peacemaking: Confrontations and Third Party Consultation.* Reading, Mass.: Addison-Wesley, 1969.

8

The Future of
the OD Profession
and Professional Ethics

INTRODUCTION

A major stumbling block in the development of an acceptable code of ethics for the OD profession is its development as a science. A common ingredient in the development of professions is the sophistication of the science of that profession. As a science evolves participants begin to form ideas about levels of expertise, skill, and standards for performance. Practitioners and scholars in a discipline are joined by consumers in forming ideas about standards for performance. Moreover, each of these interest groups contributes to scientific development. In the field of OD, the scholar's contribution is most recognizable in the formulation of conceptual frameworks, theory formulation, and testing of those theories through the application of sound research methods. Practitioners contribute by the application of concepts and theories to real world environments, while the role of a client system is to provide feedback concerning the veracity of various OD approaches. This chapter focuses on the developmental processes of OD as a science and as a profession, including the development of an ethical system for the field. The roles of scholars, practitioners, and client systems are analyzed in terms of their unique contributions. A national OD organization is proposed as the central figure in the development of the field.

DEVELOPING THE OD PROFESSION

Concerns in Developing a Science of Change

The development of the science of OD is increasingly becoming a major concern. King, Sherwood, and Manning (1978), have stressed:

> The field of OD is not now but must become a research-based science. This is probably the greatest issue confronting the field. It is not merely a question of whether we should perform research or not, but a critical demand that we must. (p. 135)

More recently Lippitt (1982) has made the point that a databased approach to organizational renewal (development) should be the goal of all change agents.

While there are numerous tools and methodologies for developing a science of change, effort is needed to bring them to fruition. At present there are three major interest groups that can contribute and play a role in the development of the science of OD. These three interest groups are the scholar/theoretician, the practitioner, and the consumer. These three groups must collaborate through the various stages that will manifest the long-term development of OD as a science. These stages are conceptualizing/developing, testing/exploring, evaluating/validating, refining/improving and integrating/generating.

Only recently have the roles of various participants in the OD process been analyzed. Mirvis and Seashore (1979) introduced the notion that role theory was a viable tool to investigate ethical dilemmas in organization research. Later, Wooten and White (1983) extended the use of role theory to explain the behavioral exchanges that occur between change agent and client system in any change effort. Going further, each interest group, scholars, practitioners, and client systems have a role to play in the development of OD as a science.

Conceptualizing/Developing

Figure 8.1 illustrates the various activities for developing the scientific base of OD. Moreover, it is a continuous process with positive actions already underway. The activity of conceptualizing/developing is where theories, models, and concepts are developed. The major responsibility for this role rests with scholars and theoreticians in the

FIG. 8.1. Long Term Development of OD as a Science

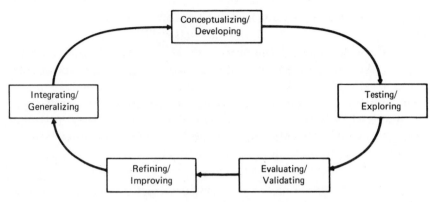

field. It could be added at this point that scholars and practitioners could be embodied in one person. The primary activity, is, however, cognitively oriented. Required behaviors at this point focus upon available knowledge of existing sciences such as the human sciences, business, and computer sciences. The available and useable knowledge is then combined in new and innovative ways that produce theories, concepts, and models, applicable to the OD field.

Testing/Exploring

The next step in the long term development of OD as a science and profession (Fig. 8.1) is testing/exploring. The activity is within the realm of the scholar. Having developed concepts and nosological networks, hypotheses need to be formulated concerning the placements or roles these concepts play in the overall theory. Moreover, these hypotheses should attempt to account for environmental influences. That is, in what settings are the theories most applicable.

Evaluating/Validating

One of the more interesting differences between the physical sciences and behavioral sciences centers around evaluation and validation. Repetition and duplication of experimentation is considered essential to the scientific process. This is not the case in the behavioral sciences, yet the long term professional and scientific development of OD must rely more upon replication of available studies, theories, and models. This process would be a shared role of the scholar, practitioner, and consumer. Scholars would continue to conduct research in laboratories where control of variables is possible so as to achieve maximum internal validity. The practitioner has a different goal and therefore, would perform his/her role differently. Activities of the practitioner would focus on maximizing external validity necessitating that evaluation/validation take place in an applied environment. The role of the consumer in this tripartite activity bifurcates along two dimensions. First, it is the organization that provides the real world environment where the problems of external validity can be dealt with. Having provided the environment for the applied research the consumer must participate fully in providing accurate feedback as to the veracity of the theories, concepts and techniques being tested.

Refining/Improving

For the process of Evaluation/Validating to reach fruition, the next step shown in Figure 8.1 (Refining/Improving) is essential. Analysis of the results of the previous steps begins the process over again. The scholar analyzes the results provided by the consumer. He/she then adapts the idea as indicated by the analysis and initiates laboratory testing of the adaptations and changes. Having achieved satisfaction of internal validity constraints, the process of Evaluating/ Validating is repeated with all three participants fulfilling their respective roles. Through this type of replication and refinement, available knowledge can be tested, refined, and improved to the point where the next step shown in Figure 8.1 can be initiated.

Integrating/Generalizing

The final activity required in the developmental process is to integrate the refined idea into the existing body of knowledge. Having accomplished refinement of the idea, OD will have a genuinely solid scientific base. This algorithmic approach can then be tested in new environments, and generalized to other problems that confront the practitioner. As these generalizations occur the continual processes shown in Figure 8.1 are initiated once again. Through this process of testing, evaluating, and replication the long-term development of OD can be accomplished. Table 8.1 summarizes the activities, required roles for the activities, and required behaviors of the actors.

TABLE 8.1. Summary of Activities, Roles, and Behaviors in the Long-Term Development of OD Science

Activity	Role Occupant	Required Behavior
Conceptualizing/ Developing	Scholar/Theoretician	Theory & concept generation through use of available knowledge
Testing/ Exploring	Scholar/Theoretician	Establish internal validity
Evaluating/ Validating	Scholar/Theoretician Practitioner Consumer	Continued Laboratory Research Establish External Validity Provide Environment; Accurate Feedback
Refining/ Improving	Scholar/Theoretician Practitioner Consumer	Modifies original idea and initiates laboratory research Retest modified idea in applied environment Provide Organizational environment and accurate feedback
Integrating/ Generalizing	Scholar/Theoretician Practitioner Consumer	Theory and concept generation through new knowledge; establish internal validity Establish External Validity Provide Environment; Accurate Feedback

Concern in Developing a Change Profession

Accompanying the development of a science of OD is the development of OD as a profession. While the field of OD has been referred to as a professional field, (Alderfer, 1977), the analysis presented in Chapter 3 suggests that much work remains before OD can legitimately accept the word profession. The Society of Personnel Administration defines a professional as:

> a person who is in an occupation requiring a high level of training and proficiency. This person has high standards of achievement with respect to acquiring unique knowledge and skills. A person who is committed to continued study, growth, and improvement for the purpose of rendering the most effective public service. The level of training, proficiency, and ethical standards are controlled by a society or association of selfgoverning members. These people maintain and improve standards and criteria for entrance and performance in the field of work or occupation (Lippitt, 1982, p. 354)

FIG. 8.2. National Organizational Development Association Organizational Chart

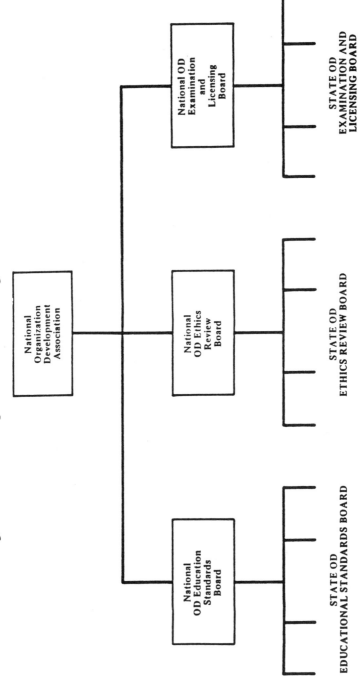

Significant progress has been made toward the recognition of OD as a profession however. Its continued long-term development can be assisted through a systematic analysis of the requisite activities, role occupants, and required behavior. Fundamental to this entire development process is a national OD agency with regional or state chapters. Figure 8.2 presents a proposed organizational chart. The proposed organization would oversee the professional growth and development of the organizational development field. The beginning of such an organization will require collaborative efforts from OD professionals representing all disciplines and existing OD organizations. Members to serve in each of the organizational functions would be elected at state/regional and national conventions. Their major function would be the development of the field through the procedures discussed below. The specific roles of the organization are discussed below.

Formulation of Professional Criteria

Figure 8.3 is an illustration of a proposed procedure for continued growth in the professionalism of OD. The establishment of professional criteria marks the beginning of this process. The question addressed in this activity would focus on a definition of the behaviors necessary to be a recognized OD professional. Scholars and practitioners from organizations such as the American Psychological Association, Academy of Management, Certified Consultants Inter-

FIG. 8.3. Long Term Development of OD as a Profession

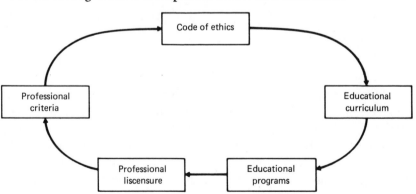

national, American Society for Training and Development, and other organizations concerned with OD will need to work closely in the development of these criteria. Equally important is participation by representative client systems who have been generally neglected when questions of concern have been addressed.

Scholars can provide a cognitive or knowledge perspective and practitioners can shed light on the application of knowledge to organizational environments, while client system representatives would provide information on acceptable consultant behaviors, as well as serve as a sounding board on the receptivity of organizations to these professional criteria.

Establishment of a Code of Ethics

The formulation of a code of ethics is a vortex around which other activities in the professional development of OD revolve. Major efforts in this are taking place in many OD organizations and while significant progress has been made much work still exists. While many OD organizations have a code of ethics (see Table 7.3) a collaborative approach is essential. Scholars, practitioners, and client systems members from the various OD organizations need to work together analyzing areas of differences and commonalities. Such an action would have as a goal a unified code of ethics for OD professionals. Moreover, review and sanctioning bodies could be established, as well as statements of appropriate actions when breaches of the code occur. With the establishment of the proposed National Organizational Development Association, national and state ethics review will assume this responsibility (see Fig. 8.2).

Specification of Educational Curriculum

The specification of educational areas will call for a joint effort of scholars, practitioners, and client systems from national and regional chapters, as well as educational institutions. Scholars, practitioners, and client systems will inventory and analyze existing knowledge, i.e., theories, concepts, and methods, to make assessments concerning their timeliness and effectiveness. Based upon their analysis, educational systems will assess current course offerings and educational procedures, discarding those that are no longer appropriate and adding new ones that the present and future profession requires. Similar to the Ethics Review Boards, this function can be assumed by National and State chapters of the Educational Standards Board (see Fig. 8.2).

Establishment of Educational Programs

The next activity in the long-term development of OD as a profession is the establishment of Educational programs. The discussion above focused on the planning of curriculum while the establishment of programs would focus on the vehicles for the educational process. As the science of OD progresses, more universities will offer advanced degrees in the field. Likewise, other training institutions such as NTL and ASTD will increase their efforts to get the science to the current and aspiring practitioner. Finally, universities as well as independent training institutions could collaborate in the development of continuing education programs to keep practitioners abreast of new developments as well as preparation for licensing examination. This too, would be a responsibility of the National and State chapters of the Educational Standards Board.

Licensing of professionals serves two major purposes. One, the process serves as a device for insuring to the client system a high level of conduct and performance; and second, it provides a means, whereby the profession can examine new entrants into the profession concerning skill, knowledge, and experience. Moreover, if the licensing body deems it appropriate, upon license renewal appropriate competency examinations can be administered to ensure that licensed individuals maintain "state of the art" competencies. State chapters comprised of scholars, practitioners, and client system members would be necessary to maintain reciprocity for OD professionals engaged in interstate activities. Collaboration between state chapters would also be necessary to maintain uniform testing and licensing procedures. Establishment of the National Organizational Development Association would result in responsibility for this activity being assumed by National and State chapters of the Examination and Licensing Board. Table 8.2 summarizes the activities, roles, and required behaviors in the long-term development of the OD profession.

TABLE 8.2. Summary of Activities, Roles, and Behaviors in the Long-Term Development of the OD Profession

Activity	Role Occupant	Required Behavior
Professional Criteria	Professional Association membership of client system	Analyze normative consultant behavior relative to descriptive consultant behavior; feedback on expected consultant behavior; and provide formulating agency with organization perspective.
Code of Ethics	Scholars Practitioners Client System	Collaboration on analysis of existing codes; Synthesis of existing codes; Establish sanction system including sanctioning body.
Educational Curriculum	Scholars Practitioners Client Systems Educational Institutions	Assess state of the art; Collaborate with educational institution; Establish course offerings including continuing education curriculum
Educa Educational Program	Scholars Practitioners Client Systems Educational Institutions	Collaboration of role occupants to provide new and innovative educational delivery systems; Develop continuing education delivery systems.
Professional Licensure	National Licensing Body State or Regional Licensing Body	Collaboration with state and regional bodies to formulate licensing examination procedures, including examination content, license renewal process, and reciprocity between state and regional chapters.

DEVELOPING A VIABLE ETHICAL SYSTEM

To develop an approach to the evolutionary process or development of professional ethical systems, it has been necessary to look at the concomitant ingredients. These are values, norms, science, laws, and eventually a code of ethics. The current stage of development is deeply involved in the science of OD in an attempt to form a necessary empirical base. All science must be grounded in and be reliant upon scientifically validated principles or ideas. (Weisbord, 1977; Friedlander, 1974; King, Sherwood and Manning, 1978).

Foregoing discussions have revealed that OD holds a relatively consistent view concerning the importance of values in the conduct of the OD process (Friedlander, 1976; Conner, 1979; Friedlander, 1976; Tichy, 1974; Farkash, 1979). Indeed, the values of the change agent vis-a-vis those of the client system form the basis for their relationship. Friedlander (1976), for example, in his discussion of nationalism, pragmatism, and existentialism points out that incongruence of these value orientations increase the probability that ethical dilemmas will occur.

Warwick and Kelman (1973), in assessing the importance of values state:

> One can distinguish four aspects of any social intervention that raise major ethical issues: (1) the choice of goals to which the change effort is directed; (2) the definition of the target of change; (3) the choice of means used to implement the intervention; and (4) the assessment of the consequences of the intervention. At each of these steps, the ethical issues that arise may involve conflicting values-questions about what values are to be maximized at the expense of what other values (p. 379)

Norms concerning OD intervention strategies have also achieved a modicum of commonality Alderfer (1976) conceptualizes these norms well. He notes:

1. The primary tasks of applied behavioral scientists working with organizations involve identifying, understanding, and changing the nature of boundaries and relationships of individuals, groups and the organization as a whole.
2. The primary goals of applied behavioral scientists working with organizations are to aid in the establishment of relevant boundaries, the opening of closed boundaries, and the movement of relationship from less to more mutuality.
3. In deciding where to start and with whom to work, a consultant should keep in mind the tendency for both the openness and closedness of boundaries to be self-sustaining.
4. An optimal structure for changing organizations consists of establishing a team (or series of teams) including insiders and outsiders.
5. The team needs to have optimally open boundaries and relationships of mutuality among team members and between the team and the system. (pp. 1632-33)

It can be seen then that values and norms for the OD profession do exist. Further refinement is necessary so that the next step in the development of an ethical system can proceed—the scientific development of OD, the development of laws, and an eventual system of ethics.

A Systematic Approach to Developing Professional Ethics

What are the events that must take place within each of the evolutionary processes? The difficult problem is compounded considerably, given the heterogeneity of OD practitioner backgrounds. These discipline areas have to be considered if the goal of acceptance of an ethical system is to be achieved. Figure 8.4 is a model for the development of an ethical system for organizational development. The five constructs comprising professional ethics are shown as benchmarks. Each major construct is accompanied by specific events that will accompany the accomplishment of that evolutionary stage.

Specification of Values

Throughout the literature concerning an operational concept of ethics, there is discussion about value systems (Zaltman and Duncan, 1976; Warwick and Kelman, 1973; Tichy, 1974). Much of the discussion centers on the question of whose values will dominate in a given intervention attempt. That is, should the client system's values prevail in deciding upon methodologies and goals, or should the values of the change agent prevail? Zaltman and Duncan (1976) hold that the important ingredient is for the client and change agent to make known the divergence of personal values, if any exists. Presumably, by allowing these feelings to surface, agreement can be reached concerning whose value system will prevail. This approach, however, perpetuates "ad hoc" ethics rather than offer a viable method for the development of a generally accepted set of values for OD.

Figure 8.4, however, takes a more macro approach to the problem in proposing that values are at the heart of any ethical system. The first step then in the development of an ethical system must be a specification of values. An alternative to the concern over whose values will prevail in a given intervention is the approach shown in Figure 8.4, which suggests that a determination of a stable system of values be specified. This could be accomplished by concerted efforts of knowledgable people in the profession formulating positions about what is good, what is right, and what is important. It is essential that specific answers to these questions be articulated. The answers to these questions cannot be situationally specific. The specifications will have to be general enough and representative of the

FIG. 8.4. Model for Development of Professional Ethics for Organizational Development

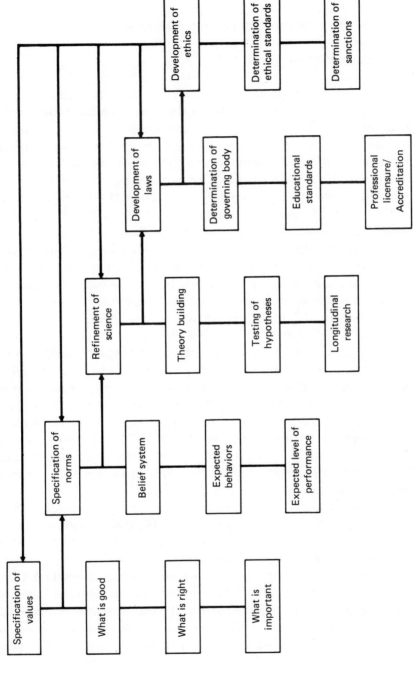

backgrounds of practitioners to allow for widespread acceptance. On the other hand, they must be specific enough to allow the interventionist to operationalize them in intervention situations.

Specifications of Norms

The values mentioned above have to be acceptable to the degree that they can be internalized. When this is accomplished, the second phase of the developmental process can mobilize. It has been noted that norms for the OD process do exist but that refinement of OD norms is needed. To illustrate why refinement of norms for the practice of OD is in fact needed, French and Bell (1978) discuss the term OD intervention. They note: "The term OD intervention refers to the range of planned programmatic activities clients and consultants participate in during the course of the organization development program." They continue, "The term OD interventions is currently being used in several different ways." They query, "Is an OD intervention something that someone does to an organization, or is it something that is going on, that is, an activity?" (p. 101).

French and Bell (1978) point out three ways that the term OD intervention is perceived. First, it is something an external agent does to the client system. Second, it sometimes means or is used to refer to a method or intervention technique. Finally, the term OD intervention may be applied to different levels of activity. Thus, a norm has been established concerning what OD intervention is in the general sense, however, the lack of refinement concerns a lack of specificity about intervention. French and Bell (1978) sum it up by pointing out that "all of these are correct uses of the term intervention, but they relate to different levels of abstraction and can thus be confusing at times" (p. 102).

A systematic analysis of the somewhat ambiguous perception or definition points to three components in the specification of norms, regarding OD intervention. These are belief systems, expected behaviors, and expected levels of performance.

At the outset of this phase, belief systems play a very important role. These belief systems can be compared to ascertain the expected behaviors of the interventionist and of the client system. Actually, an enumeration of expected behaviors for interventionists has to be formulated as a function of the expected behaviors of the client system.

Having decided upon the expected behaviors, expected levels of performance will begin to emerge. Currently, a change agent must make decisions about levels of performance on an ad hoc basis due to a lack of refinement of norms. Once decisions about levels of performance and behavior are established, a reference point has been established thereby adding impetus to the eventual formulation of an acceptable ethical system.

Refinement of the Science of Organizational Development

Figure 8.4 depicts where refinement of a science sequences with regard to the development of an ethical system for OD. As shown, this phase cannot reach fruition until values and norms have been fully developed and specified. These developments, when they occur, will enhance the scientific development of OD. Current critiques of the science of OD point to some disturbing facts. White and Mitchell (1976) said:

> The measures are subject to halo errors and poor reliability. The designs are frequently inadequate for making causal inferences. Statistical comparisons are weak and infrequently used. Finally, Hawthorne and experimenter bias effects provide highly plausible alternative hypotheses. Thus one is left with studies reporting substantial support for OD efforts, but little feeling of confidence in the way in which the support was generated. (p. 70)

To overcome these weaknesses, White and Mitchell (1976) offered a four step approach: "(1) Development of a classification system of organizational variables, (2) construction of hypotheses relating to the OD field, (3) theory building, and (4) theory testing."

The model presented in Figure 8.4 presents a somewhat different view. There is a science of OD that has emerged in the recent works of Lippitt, 1982; French and Bell, 1978; however, this base is in need of refinement. King, et al. (1978) takes a similar position by advocating that OD's research face be expanded. The scientific refinement of OD has accomplished theory building to a great degree. The next step that needs to be accomplished is the formulation of hypotheses about the relationships that comprise these theories for their eventual longitudinal testing.

This task can be accomplished using both field and laboratory designs. Development of an ethical system is as dependent upon empiricism as is the development of the parent science of OD. A route should be followed such as Kuhn (1970) has proposed for the development of a scientific paradigm. Efforts should be made to develop the scientific paradigm in the context of its applied environment (Dubin, 1969).

Development of Laws

In the preceding chapter the published ethical codes of various professional organizations engaged in the practice of OD were analyzed according to five criteria. Collaboration among these organizations has not transpired at this time; however, it will be necessary for representatives from these bodies to work together to develop laws for the OD profession. Figure 8.4 shows that three steps are necessary for the development of laws. They are: (1) determination of a governing body; (2) establishment of educational standards; and (3) professional licensure and accreditation.

The first step in the development of laws in producing an ethical system will be the determination of a governing body. The participants should be representative of practitioners and scholars from the related disciplines, e.g., the American Psychological Association, The American Society of Personnel Administrators, the Academy of Management/OD Division, etc. This body would concern itself with developing educational standards and establishing criteria for licensing and accreditation of OD consultants. This interdisciplinary governing body should be involved in assisting colleges and universities in curriculum construction for adherence to educational standards for eventual licensing and accreditation of students. Important to the success of requiring a license and accreditation to practice as a consultant would be the cooperation of client systems. One way to insure this cooperation would be through stringent licensing and accreditation requirements. This would insure the client system of a consistently high level of professionalism and expertise.

Development of Ethics

The development of an ethical system is very much dependent upon the occurrence of values and norms specification, as well as the refinement of the science and development of the laws. Based upon values, norms, science, and laws, a determination of ethical standards would be possible. The inherent interaction of values, norms, science, and laws cannot be understated as a necessary ingredient for the development of a system of professional ethics. It then appears necessary that the development of OD as a science be in concert with established norms and procedures. The natural outgrowth of this kind of a balanced developmental process will be a specification of a system of ethics for OD that can be accepted by OD interventionists, their particular science of origin notwithstanding. Moreover, this will aid the development of sanction systems and monitoring mechanisms sensitive to acute deviations.

The model for the development of professional ethics in OD shown in Figure 8.4 suggests the use of OD techniques in the development of OD itself. It suggests, that an action research approach be utilized involving representative groups to assist in the clarification and specification of the values and norms of OD and to assist in the establishment of criteria for its development as a science. This group would also be responsible for the development of its laws, monitoring processes, and the eventual development of the content and maintenance of an ethical system. If OD is to be a true discipline, then it must use a disciplined approach to its development.

Future Ethical Concerns

Perhaps the most difficult task facing professional ethicists is to anticipate with any accuracy the ethical questions OD professionals will face during the years remaining in the decade of the 80s and beyond. As the science of the field becomes more sophisticated, what is now speculation will become amenable to assessment through statistical probabilities. Current organizational and social events however, provide some clues about future ethical considerations. First, and perhaps what is most certain, is the enduring nature of change. Lippitt (1982) explains:

> No person or group of persons, however empowered, can prevent change from occurring. At best, they can only hasten or delay it. More important, they can cope with change at all only if they are aware of its nature and probable effect. In this sense, those responsible for the management of our organizations are faced with extraordinary difficulties in being always correctly informed and situationally knowledgeable. Organizational changes faithfully reflect the needs and interests of some

of the people, but not necessarily all of them; therefore, they inevitably produce inequities. Since everything is the result of a change, competent managers cannot afford to overlook any change whatsoever, because every change is a seed from which some part of tomorrow's organization will grow. (p. 385)

Given this inevitability, future interventionists, similar to present interventionists, will confront the question of the ethicality of change itself. That is, the depth of an intervention sometimes strikes at the very heart of the human and organizational interaction. French and Bell (1978) assess the depth that an intervention might require.

. . . the initial vehicle for organization development efforts—for improvements in any or all of the organizational subsystems—tends to be an intervention in the human-social and the structural subsystems. . . . [T]here is an immediate interrelated impact between the human-social and the structural subsystem. (p. 43)

The OD professional must continue then to be sensitive to the effects that organization development processes have on organization participants. It appears that questions of informed consent will continue both in the short run and the long run.

A move in the organizational value orientations seems to have taken root and will continue. Organizations have moved from productivity/efficiency to humanism to a hybrid or systems value orientation. The OD consultant of the future will be faced with questions of ethicality concerning variances in personal value system and organizational value systems. He/she as any other professional must render services when requested thus confronting issues of defining who the client is. It has been noted above that there is in OD some value consensus. However, the developing profession must remain sensitive to the changing values of society. What organizations of today need and expect may differ from the needs and expectations of future organizations and their participants. A frequent criticism of the medical and law professions is that certain segments of society receive better medical care and better legal assistance as a function of the ability to pay for these services. The OD consultant of the 80s will, undoubtedly, face this question. Organizations that can afford OD services will benefit and prosper while others without the resources will be unable to deal with problems that confront them.

The phenomenal growth and sophistication of computer technology will also create new ethical challenges for the OD consultants. With this sophistication will come more organizational evaluation. More data will be generated about organizational participants creating a myriad of ethical questions about ownership of data and confidentiality. The recent incidents of intersystem intrusion creates new questions for the interventionist concerning confidentiality of data.

Moreover, as the sophistication of the field continues in the 80s more advanced computer technology will assist in the development of OD as a science. The profession must guard against the pendulum moving from humanism to empiricism to the degree that humanism is shunted aside in a search for refined research.

The remaining 80s and beyond will see increased multinational organizational growth. Surely demand for OD services will experience true internationalism. How will OD efforts in one subsystem affect operations in another subsystem. Prevailing value and ethics vary extensively from one culture to another. How will the OD community respond to these challenges? It seems certain that the field of organizational development will experience growth and expansion. Development of an ethical system or code for OD professionals will be faced with questions such as these. It is necessary, however that professional bodies collaborate and develop a comprehensive statement that all OD professionals will accept.

SUMMARY

This chapter has dealt with two major issues of the field of OD—developing both the OD profession and a viable ethical system. Concerns for developing a science of change were discussed. The five major activities for achieving this goal are: conceptualizing/developing, testing exploring, evaluating/validating, refining/improving, and integrating/generalizing. Concerns for developing a change profession centered on: formulation of professional criteria, establishment of a code of ethics, specification of educational criteria, and establishment of educational programs. Finally, a method for the developing of a system of ethics for OD was proposed. It was proposed that a national OD organization with area chapters be established with the responsibility to oversee the development and maintenance of the profession through continued development of scientific, educational, and professional standards with representation from schools, practitioner, and client system groups. This comprehensive organization would focus upon concerns confronting OD currently, as well as deal with the challenges of the 80s and beyond.

NOTES

Alderfer, C. P. "Organizational Development." *Annual Review of Psychology* 28, 1977, 197-283.

Alderfer, C. P. "Change Processes in Organizations." In M. D. Dunnette (ed.), *Handbook of Industrial Organizational Psychology*. Chicago: Rand McNally, 1976.

Conner, P. E. "A Critical Inquiry in Some Assumptions and Values Characterizing OD." *The Academy of Management Review* 2, 1979, 635-44.

Dubin, R. *Theory Building*. New York: The Free Press, 1969.

Farkash, A. *An Empirical Investigation of Organizational Development Belief, Activities, and Outcomes*. Selected Paper no. 8. Madison, Wis.: American Society for Training and Development, 1979.

French, W. H. and Bell, C. H., Jr., *Organizational Development*. Englewood Cliffs, N.J.: Prentice-Hall, 1978.

Friedlander, F. *Purpose and Values in OD: Toward Personal Theory and Practice*. Madison, Wis.: American Society for Training and Development, 1976.

Friedlander, F. "OD Reaches Adolescence: An Exploration of its Underlying Values." *Journal of Applied Behavior Science* 12, no. 1, 1976, 7-12.

Friedlander, F. and Brown, L. D. "Organization Development." *Annual Review of Psychology* 25, 1974, 313-41.

Huse, E. *Organizational Development and Change*. St. Paul: West, 1975.

King, D. C., Sherwood, J. J. and Manning, M. R. "OD Research Base: How To Expand and Utilize It." In W. W. Burke, *The Cutting Edge: Current Theory and Practice in Organization Development*. La Jolla, Cal.: University Associates, 1978.

Kuhn, T. S. *The Structure of Scientific Revolutions.* Chicago: The University of Chicago Press, 1970.

Lippitt, G. L. *Organization Renewal: A Holistic Approach to Organization Development.* 2nd ed. Englewood Cliffs, N.J.: Prentice-Hall, 1982.

Margulies, M. and Raia, A. *Conceptual Foundations of Organizational Development.* New York: McGraw-Hill, 1978.

Mirvis, P. H. and Seashore, S. E., "Being Ethical in Organizational Research." *American Psychologist* 34, no. 9, 1979, 766-780.

Tichy, N. "Agents of Planned Change: Congruence of Values, Cognitions, and Action." *Administrative Science Quarterly* 19, no. 2, 1974, 164–82.

Warwick, D. P. and Kelman, H. C. "Ethics Issues in Social Intervention." In G. Zaltman (ed.), *Processes and Phenomena of Social Change.* New York: Wiley-Interscience, 1973.

Weisbord, M. R. How Do You Know If It Works If You Don't Know What It Is? *O.D. Practitioner* 9, 1977, 1-3.

White, S. E. and Mitchell, T. R. "Organization Development: A Review of Research Content and Research Design." *The Academy of Management Review* 2, 1976, 53-73.

Wooten, K. C. and White, L. P. "Ethical Problems in the Practice of Organization Development." *Training and Development Journal*, April, 1983, 16-23.

Zaltman, G. and Duncan, R. "Ethics in Social Change." In G. Zaltman and R. Duncan (eds.), *Strategies for Planned Change.* New York: John Wiley and Sons, 1976.

Index

Index

About the Authors

LOUIS P. WHITE is Associate Professor of Management and the Director of Programs in Management and Marketing, University of Houston-Clear Lake. He has held positions as Assistant Dean, College of Education, University of South Florida; and Plant Manager, and was on the Board of Directors, Photoengraving Inc., Tampa, Florida.

Dr. White is an active consultant in the public and private sectors and is a member of the panel of the American Arbitration Association. He is the author of 25 professional papers and articles that have appeared in publications such as the *Academy of Management Review*, the *Training and Development Journal*, and *Gaming and Simulation*.

Dr. White received his Ph.D. in Industrial Psychology from the University of South Florida, where he served on the faculty.

KEVIN C. WOOTEN is Manager of Training and Development at Entex, Inc. in Houston, Texas. Since 1980, he has been responsible for extensive employee, supervisory, and management development efforts, as well as long-range human resource planning. Concurrently, he has served as adjunct faculty for the School of Business at the University of Houston-Clear Lake, teaching undergraduate and graduate classes in Industrial Management.

Mr. Wooten has presented numerous papers and published frequently in the area of employee and organizational development. His articles have appeared in the *Training and Development Journal*, *Academy of Management Review*, and *Gaming and Simulation*.

Mr. Wooten holds a B.A. in Psychology and an M.A. in Behavioral Science from the University of Houston-Clear Lake. His memberships include the American Psychological Association, American Society for Training and Development, Human Resource Planning Society, and the International Registry of Organizational Development Professionals.